FUTURE POLITY

FUTURE POLITY

Using Autonomous Policymaking to
Shape Progressive Societies

MOHAMED AL JNEIBI

HOUNDSTOOTH
PRESS

COPYRIGHT © 2024 MOHAMED AL JNEIBI
All rights reserved.

FUTURE POLITY
Using Autonomous Policymaking to Shape Progressive Societies
First Edition

ISBN	978-1-5445-4650-6	*Hardcover*
	978-1-5445-4649-0	*Paperback*
	978-1-5445-4651-3	*Ebook*
	978-1-5445-4652-0	*Audiobook*

CONTENTS

Introduction **ix**

Chapter 1. The Allegory of Good and Bad Government **1**
Chapter 2. Why Humans Make Bad Policies **15**
Chapter 3. The Challenge of Complexity **33**
Chapter 4. Letting Machines Take Control **63**
Chapter 5. Why Intelligent Systems Are the Best Bet for Our Future **83**
Chapter 6. What Exactly Do We Mean by Artificial Intelligence Anyway? **99**
Chapter 7. Machines That Teach Themselves **119**
Chapter 8. When AI Goes Wrong **153**
Chapter 9. Singapore: Building a Nation from Scratch **185**
Chapter 10. The Power of Policy **207**
Chapter 11. Navigating the Labyrinth of AI and Public Policy **239**

Acknowledgements **249**
Further Reading **251**

INTRODUCTION

A few years ago, while working on my master's degree in global public policy, much of the focus I had placed on the various research areas normally fell within the realm of data. I had posted most of my thinking on what data could do better for policy. These general questions included: "How could data be used in situations that would uplift and elevate the overall greater good?" and "How could we continuously uplift the information accessibility to better support informed decisions made within the local constituencies that are served?"

Policy making is a vast space, and one that is quite experiential in nature. While general counsel and consensus building are the preferred hallmarks of well-informed policy drafts, today, there is a growing acknowledgment that we have expanded our ability to interact with the same data sets by many folds, moving beyond the once "data-centric or -driven" approach. Policy development and analysis has a likely pathway into becoming a commoditized practice in the realm of various generative artificial intelligence developments that are enhancing the condition of so many facets of society. Most of which have intertwining dependencies to modern policies addressing the unique problems that were resolved.

One of this book's core arguments is we may soon deliver "policy kits" to help developing economies put policies into place that will best deliver core governmental objectives. Ministers may soon set their vision on central issues—trade, education, healthcare, transport, taxation—then plug in data and let machines advise them as to the policies that will produce the required result, rather than lurching from one poorly thought-through policy to the next and coping with the consequences of each reversal of fortune.

This may sound like the stuff of science fiction, but a great deal of current technology was as well until just a short time ago. Before we look at new technologies and how they can transform how policies are made and implemented, we must first examine some of the more obvious frailties and fallibilities of human policymaking.

The main concern of this book is with *distributive* policies—the use of public funds to increase the common good—because there is a great deal of evidence showing that humans are notably bad at distributing public goods in the most efficient way. We have glaring examples of public money being spent in ways that are deeply inefficient and occasionally downright corrupt. Which is precisely why we would do well to consider automating a great deal of our policymaking—handing it over to machines—to make it more efficient and less corrupt, and to bring big data and computing power to bear on policy areas that currently rely on partially informed and fallible human policymakers.

How could machine intelligence help resolve a policy issue as complex and highly charged as India's agricultural policy? If the politicians can't fix this, is there any way a machine can help? When we note machine intelligence in the book, I am using a general subset of the great artificial intelligence sciences that can support predictions-based analysis in a variety of scenarios, not least of which is policy development.

The central premise of this book is that **machine intelligence** will help governments and their constituents in the formulation and implementation of policy. As people become more aware of such capabilities and their benefits, they will become more comfortable allowing machines to decide on their behalf. Artificial intelligence systems can run unimaginable numbers of scenarios using equally unthinkable amounts of data. When machine intelligence tells us, "This is the most likely outcome" or "This is the most helpful outcome given the current objective and within the chosen parameters," we will come to accept that as our new truth—our hypertruth.

These hypertruths can create far more effective policies by the governments of the future—both for developed and, importantly, for developing economies.

Economic and social policy is complex, but it is not incomprehensible: we understand the levers we plan to utilize and the outcomes we desire. In the past, we have had no alternative but to put policies in place and hope they work out the way we intended—which they often do not. Machine intelligence will enable us to analyze far more data and to run huge numbers of scenarios in search of optimal results and unforeseen and unwanted consequences arising from proposed policies, greatly improving the quality of policymaking.

Human behavior is of course prone to bias and irrationality, and it might be argued that machine intelligence can never cope with human beings' sheer stubbornness and their tendency to take issue with even the most enlightened and effective policies. But we are also gaining, for the first time in history, huge amounts of data on how human beings behave at an astonishing level of granularity, allowing us to make increasingly accurate predictions about how people will respond in the future in a wide range of scenarios.

In the next chapter, I delve into the allegory of good and bad government, using the historical example of Siena in the

Middle Ages. This story illustrates the impact of well-crafted policies and the dire consequences of poor governance. By understanding the principles that guided the Noveschi in medieval Siena, we can draw parallels to our current technological advancements and envision a future where AI enhances policymaking for the common good.

As we embark on this journey, keep in mind the transformative potential of AI in policymaking. Just as Siena's leaders used their resources and knowledge to build a thriving city, we can harness the power of AI to create policies that foster prosperity, equity, and beauty in our societies.

I further continue within the book to highlight examples of policies that were crafted with both leading or revolutionary practices, or with the help of technology. Policy development at its core listens to the conditions of the current state, and with that, many nation states have varying degrees of innovative thinking and logic to address the pressing key local challenges of the day.

This book may not provide an ideal answer on how we will navigate the future state of policy development, but it will give you a deeper understanding of how unique challenges were resolved in different ways. I will reference many historical points, sometimes at great lengths, to highlight the formulation of key driving principles used by the relevant policy thinkers of the time. Understanding the historical events that shaped the thinking of problem solvers is crucial to many approaches in this context.

This book is not about the benefits of particular forms of government. It is about the benefits of good policy. I intend to make the case we will rely more on machine intelligence not simply to *inform* policy—which is becoming common as we use big data to give us new insights into complex areas and reveal hidden trends and patterns—but also to *make decisions about* policy on our behalf.

CHAPTER 1
THE ALLEGORY OF GOOD AND BAD GOVERNMENT

IN THE MIDDLE AGES, SIENA—NESTLED IN THE HILLY northwestern region of Tuscany, Italy—was one of the most important cities in Europe. Not only a major banking center, it was also home to one of the world's oldest universities—the Studium Senese, founded in 1240—and the birthplace of several important early Renaissance artists.

In the immediate aftermath of the fall of the Western Roman Empire in 476 CE, the Lombards ruled most of what is now Italy. In the eighth century, the King of the Franks, Charlemagne, defeated them. He united Western and Central Europe for the first time since the Romans into what would become known as the Holy Roman Empire.

Charlemagne may have been the nominal ruler of northern Italy, but the actual power in Tuscany lay in the hands of various aristocratic families. The society was feudal, though several of the great city-states of Italy—Venice, Milan, Florence, Lucca, Siena, and several more—were emerging as trading centers too large and sophisticated to be contained within the old feudal model.

In 1125, the commune of Siena created a new republic, governed by an elected Consul—a position that had been the most senior-elected public office of the old Roman Republic prior to imperial rule by the Caesars. The local nobility still held key powers in the surrounding lands while the Bishop of Siena, drawing his authority from the Pope in Rome, was the city's governor. But in 1167, Sienna declared itself to be independent of Rome; the city issued a written constitution in 1179. Having thrived on the growing wool trade, profits from wool and agriculture were used to create lending institutions. The development of such embryonic institutions would lead to the establishment of the Banca Monte dei Paschi, one of the world's oldest banks (founded in 1472).

THE BUILDING OF A MEDIEVAL POLICYMAKING INFRASTRUCTURE

In 1286, a new government took over from the old consular government. The Noveschi, a new political class of bankers and wealthy merchants, established a system of government by selecting nine council members ("The Nine") through a lottery from their own members. Each council served for only two months before the selection of nine new members. The pool of people from whom The Nine could be selected deliberately excluded the feudal nobility since there was a fear that powerful families might regain power. Avoiding a reassertion of pre-republican "tyranny" lay at the heart of the Noveschi period of government.

Also excluded from The Nine were the "lower crafts:" stonemasons, blacksmiths, glassworkers, and the like, while professionals such as physicians, lawyers, and notaries could serve in the Council of the Bell—a citizen council of 300 summoned to session by town criers and the ringing of bells in the Palazzo Publico, Siena's magnificent center of government built by the Noveschi between 1297 and 1308. Members of the old feudal nobility could also serve on the Council of the Bell, though the late Richard Ingersoll, an architectural historian at Rice University in the United States, argues in an archived lecture that the Council of the Bell "rubber stamped all policies coming from the Noveschi."[1]

---

1   Richard Ingersoll, "Lecture 10: The Uses of Decorum," Rice University (Arch 343: Cities in History), last modified October 5, 1995, https://web.archive.org/web/20090316063951/http:/www.owlnet.rice.edu/~arch343/lecture10.html.

To protect The Nine from outside influence—what we might now call lobbying but in medieval society was far more likely to involve straightforward bribery and corruption—members of The Nine lived in the Palazzo Publico for the duration of their two-month term of office.

The Noveschi had set out to introduce technocracy of "hard-headed businessmen." The system insulated The Nine from corruption at the hands of wealthy individuals or businesses hoping for lucrative government contracts via physical isolation in the Palazzo and rapid turnover. Though the 300 members of the Council of the Bell represented a check on the power of The Nine, the Noveschi government was far from democratic. What it became was an efficient system for generating and implementing policy, with the Noveschi very much focused on Siena's economic development. For posterity's sake, the medieval governors of Siena also believed a thriving city was to be distinguished by the beauty of its architecture and art, not just the health and wealth of its citizens.

POLICYMAKING IN A NEW AGE

This book is about policy and the future of policymaking. Specifically, it will explore how policymaking might look in a future where we have unprecedented amounts of data about people's lives and behaviors available, along with new techniques like artificial intelligence (AI) that allow for the analysis of data in ways that go far beyond human capabilities. We are now, for the first time in history, able to evaluate unimaginable volumes of data at unthinkable speeds to detect trends and patterns that are indiscernible to merely human analysis.

Policymaking should shape future behaviors and outcomes based on overall objectives for societies. Big data can augment current understanding of how those societies work—and how to meet the challenges. Advancing computing power is capable of significantly improving and even transforming the quality of our policymaking.

THE ANCIENT ART OF POLICYMAKING

The sole purpose of policy—no matter whether developed by humans or computers enabled with AI—is to improve people's lives. The policies of The Nine in medieval Siena offer an excellent example of the benefits of good policymaking. The series of three frescoes found in the Sala dei Nove ("Salon of The Nine") is part of the Palazzo Publico. The Noveschi commissioned the *Allegory of Good and Bad Government*, which the great Sienese artist Ambrogio Lorenzetti painted between 1338 and 1339.

They cover three walls of the Sala dei Nove and depict a scene of horror and chaos, with a witch-like female figure flying above the walls of a city and ravaged countryside, brandishing a long sword in her raised right hand. She is Timor (Fear), skin blackened, teeth bared, with the face of a corpse. She carries a legend in her left hand that reads:

> Because each person seeks only their own good, Tyranny subjects Justice in this city. Wherefore, along this road, nobody passes without fearing for his life, since there are robberies outside and inside the city gates.

To the far right, the figure of Tyranny is devil-like, with horns and fangs, surrounded by Avarice, Pride, Vainglory, Cruelty, Treason, Furor, Division, and War. At the feet of Tyranny is the bound and downcast figure of Justice lying on the ground, without her crown, her hair loose and disheveled. The legend reads:

> There, where Justice is bound no one is ever in accord for the Common Good...Therefore, it is fitting that Tyranny prevails. She [Tyranny], in order to carry out her iniquity, neither wills nor acts in disaccord with the filthy nature of the Vices, who are shown here conjoined with her.[2]

---

2 Randolph Starn, *Ambrogio Lorenzetti: The Palazzo Publico, Siena* (New York: George Braziller Inc., 1994), 99.

The fresco on the north wall depicts "The Virtues of Good Government" with brighter colors. To the left, beneath the figure of Wisdom, Justice sits regally on her throne. Next to her, justice is being done and being seen to be done, with a winged angel decapitating one unfortunate with a sword while rewarding a second kneeling figure with a crown. To the left, another angel distributes rewards to two worthy citizens, a bale of cloth to one and what may be a metalworker's spear and a weaver's distaff to another. Further to the left sits the magisterial, white-bearded figure of the Common Good, flanked by the virtues of Peace, Fortitude, Prudence, Magnanimity, Temperance, and Justice. Hovering over the scene are the "theological virtues" of Faith, Charity, and Hope.

The moral is clear. As a legend from "The Virtues of Good Government" proclaims:

> The holy Virtue [Justice], wherever she rules, induces to unity the many souls and they, gathered together for such a purpose, make the Common Good their Lord; and he, in order to govern his state, chooses never to turn his eyes from the resplendent faces of the Virtues who sit around him. Therefore, to him in triumph are offered taxes, tributes and lordship of towns.

Indeed, taxes rewarded the Noveschi for their virtuous behavior. In 1320, they introduced an income tax, assessing the value of citizens' properties and levying appropriate taxes (Florence later took this idea up). The Noveschi also introduced a form of public debt.

Unlike her nearby rival Florence, built on the banks of the mighty Arno River, Siena has very little natural supply of water. The Noveschi built miles of tunnels to bring water to some fifty newly built public fountains. Three officials, called praetors and anointed for one-year terms, supervised the public works and enforced building codes and standards. They ensured that smaller streets had a minimum width of nine feet, while major ones had to be at least twenty-two feet wide. The Palazzo Publico, along with many of the city's greater and lesser houses, used Siena's characteristic red bricks for construction. The government established a monopoly on their manufacture to impose quality standards and ensure consistency in building materials.

That same red brick paves Siena's world-famous central square, the Piazza del Campo, laid out in a herringbone fashion. Long insets of white travertine limestone divide the square's bricks into nine sections, radiating out from the front of the Palazzo Publico like a fan or a scallop shell. The great houses—the palazzi signorii—that line the edges of the square to this day were home to Siena's noble families.

A decree mandated that these houses should have a unified roofline, ensuring that no one house stood out from or dominated others. This decision gave the whole square an architectural and aesthetic integrity that helps explain its reputation as one of Europe's greatest medieval squares.

Great nobles had lived in tower houses, basically fortified stone towers that served as both the family home and a power base to defend and dominate the surrounding area. By doing away with competing tower houses, Siena imposed symbolic egalitarianism on its cityscape. In his lecture, Ingersoll quotes the city's medieval statutes, which say:

> ...it responds to the beauty of the city of Siena and to the satisfaction of almost all people of the same city that any edifices that are to be made anew anywhere along the public thoroughfares...proceed in line with the existent buildings and on[e] building not stand out beyond another, but they shall be disposed and arranged equally so as to be of the greatest beauty for the city.[3]

For the Noveschi, Siena should not only be well-run and efficiently designed—with plentiful water and streets wide enough for people and animals to pass and fresh air to

---

3   Ingersoll, "Lecture 10."

circulate—it should also be *beautiful*. This is why the astonishing art of the period adorned the interiors of public buildings. In 1316, a notary working in the Palazzo Publico noted that some of the frescoes in the Palazzo (before Lorenzetti's frescoes were painted) were "a delight to the eye, a joy to the heart, and a pleasure to all the senses."[4] The Noveschi also set in train the rebuilding of Siena's cathedral and constructed a large hospital, the Santa Maria della Scala.

The Noveschi rule represents Siena's golden age, although it was on the verge of ending. When members of The Nine chose each other by lot every two months from the pool of "good and lawful merchants," they pledged to strive for "the conservation, augmentation, and magnificence of the present regime."[5] They succeeded for a time but were fatally hampered by the city's lack of water. The wool industry and agriculture, the powerhouses of medieval economies, both needed water, with the manufacture of cloth, in particular, requiring huge volumes. It is estimated that Siena's great rival, Florence—plentifully supplied by the Arno—employed as many people in the wool industry during this period as there were inhabitants of Siena.[6] The Arno also gave Florence direct access to the sea to export

---

4   Starn, *Ambrogio Lorenzetti*, 12.
5   Starn, *Ambrogio Lorenzetti*, 15.
6   Starn, *Ambrogio Lorenzetti*, 13.

finished goods and import essentials and luxuries. Competing with Florence had always been a necessity and a struggle for Siena.

In 1348, the Black Death arrived, killing one-third of Siena's presumed fifty thousand citizens in one year. The city never fully recovered. In 1355, Holy Roman Emperor Charles IV arrived in Siena to remind people that these were theoretically his territories, triggering uprisings against the Noveschi by the nobility and the *popolo*, who felt their taxes were used to support the comfortable lifestyles of the ruling merchant class. It is worth noting that the *popolo* were well-to-do citizens of Siena, not some revolutionary rabble, who had been largely excluded from what was, in effect, the elite banking/merchant oligarchy imposed by the Noveschi.

The *popolo* were triumphant, expelling all families associated with the Noveschi. Some republican institutions clung to life in the coming decades, with the Noveschi allowed to return in the mid-fifteenth century and resume their activities as a political faction. They returned to power in 1487 under Pandolfo Petrucci, who used his new political power and family's wealth to seize individual control in 1500 and rule as a despot. He survived many political intrigues (both France and Spain invaded Italy and forged various alliances) and an assassination attempt by the infamous Cesare Borgia, whom Petrucci had crossed. On Borgia's death, Petrucci became one of Italy's most powerful men. The Sienese economy prospered under him, and his family ruled Siena until 1524. Siena finally fell to its great rival Florence, then in alliance with Spain, in 1555.

GOOD POLICY IS TIMELESS

Good policies can create prosperity and plenty, improve the quality of people's lives, and help build thriving and even beautiful environments in which people can live good lives. Bad policies cannot create such optimal conditions and can even lead to the collapse of civilized society, as in Lorenzetti's depiction of "The City State Under Tyranny."

But policymaking is difficult. The most advanced political systems introduce new policies that have unintended consequences or are plain misguided (I will explore several examples in the book). Ministers of developing economies may lack policymaking expertise and experience, and politicians in both advanced and developing economies are fallible, keen to please their various constituencies, and open to petty or grand corruption.

In the twenty-first century, we have new technologies at our disposal: the potential use of various forms of artificial intelligence to analyze the vast amounts of data available to us about our behaviors and interactions with our fellow citizens and environments. These technologies offer us a chance to create scientific policies and use technology to supplement or even replace our flawed human abilities.

CHAPTER 2
WHY HUMANS MAKE BAD POLICIES

I**N 2014, THE WEBSITE MILITARY.COM—A WEBSITE** for members and veterans of the US military—ran the memorable headline, "Congress Again Buys Abrams Tanks the Army Doesn't Want." The M1 Abrams tank was introduced as America's main battle tank in 1980 and has since seen two new iterations, the M1A1 and the M1A2, and is manufactured at the Lima Army Tank Plant in Ohio.

This was not the first time Congress had voted to build tanks the army did not want. In 2012, army officials testified at various congressional hearings about a desire to suspend tank building and upgrades. US Army Chief of Staff General Ray Odierno stated, "We don't need tanks. Our tank fleet is two and a half years old on average now. We're in good shape and these are additional tanks that we don't need." He argued the army wanted to become a lighter force and that production lines at Lima could be kept open and essential skills retained through the continued sales of Abrams tanks to other countries—an export version of the tank sold to Egypt, Kuwait, Saudi Arabia, Australia, and Iraq. Despite the general's recommendation, Congress ordered $183 million of upgrades. "If we had our choice, we would use that money differently," Odierno told the Associated Press.

How can government policy result in the allocation of huge amounts of funding for unwanted projects—such as tanks the army does not want? Two answers exist for that question: one encompasses the various policies implemented by governments, and the other entails the corrupt motivations for politicians in any form of representative government.

The American political scientist Theodore J. Lowi put government policy on the map in 1972. He believed "policies determine politics," which he saw as "the very opposite of the typical perspective in political science."[1] He meant that political science was far more focused on the glamorous business of "politics" than it was on the apparently unglamorous business of policymaking.

---

1 Theodore J. Lowi, "Four Systems of Policy, Politics, and Choice," *Public Administration Review* 32, no. 4 (July–August 1972): 299, https://doi.org/10.2307/974990.

Lowi thought that setting up a classification of the different types of government policy would provide more focus to the field. His classification of four types of policy—distributive, redistributive, regulatory, and constituent—still provides the foundation for the modern study of policymaking.

- Distributive policies are designed to fund beneficial projects. Such policies may only impact certain segments of society, but the overall intent is to provide for the common good. Examples are spending on education, research, defense, road building, urban renewal, sewage treatment, etc.

- Redistributive policies aim to change the distribution of various resources throughout society to achieve a more equal society. Progressive taxation is perhaps the definitive example of redistributive policy: taxing wealthier citizens provides funds for other redistributive policies, such as welfare, housing, or healthcare programs that benefit less wealthy citizens.

- Regulatory policies should prevent antisocial behaviors or correct market failures and create a more level playing field for all citizens. Examples are crime prevention, rules on unfair competition and misleading advertising, safety and quality standards for consumer goods, food and drug safety laws, etc.

- Constituent policies set rules about how governments make rules and might involve changes to the constitution, setting up a new government agency, or new rules affecting the legislative process.

Of these, redistributive policies are the most overtly "political" because they fit into the spectrum of political beliefs, which spans the extremes of some form of communism or revolutionary socialism and radical laissez-faire or libertarian ideologies. They create a framework within which other policymaking takes place, with members of political parties having to decide where they stand on that spectrum of beliefs.

The politicians who make policy have various constituencies, the people they need to please if they are to remain in power. Liberal democracies, interestingly, offer an excellent example of just how complex and murky that web of various constituencies can become.

Elected politicians are most obviously accountable to the people who voted for them, in the most straightforward sense, their "constituency." Lawmakers have to be seen as using their influence in government—however great or small—in ways that benefit the people in their constituency. They need to be seen at least fulfilling the promises made on the campaign trail.

But politicians have other, less obvious, constituencies. There will be significant industries and other organizations within a politician's physical constituency that provide jobs and taxes that help the constituency flourish. It is important for a politician to be perceived as promoting policies in the best interest of these organizations. There may also be opportunities to direct government funds toward these industries and organizations in a more direct sense.

Donors from inside or outside the politician's constituency, including industries and organizations, also supported a politician's career in the politician's constituency. These various donors will have decided that the politician is to advance their interests, either in the general sense of following the donors' preferred political direction or, again, in the specific sense of helping implement policies that directly benefit the donor. A politician known to be supportive of a particular industry affected by government legislation, for example, might get support from that industry even when based outside their geographical constituency. The politician, again, needs to be seen as acting in ways that further these donors' interests, rewarding them for their financial support.

Politicians have yet another constituency: fellow politicians. They can support colleagues by promising their vote for some piece of policy that colleagues are especially keen to pass, and they can make that vote dependent on support for their own favored policies. The word for this in American politics is "logrolling," thought to derive from the practice of frontier communities coming together to cut down trees and roll the harvested timber to where log cabins were to be built in the wilderness or to build a supply of firewood for the winter. In political terms, logrolling means a similar exchange of favors: "I'll vote for your bill if you'll vote for mine—or if there is something in your bill that benefits my constituents."

Another term that has entered the American political vernacular is "pork-barrel politics." No one is sure where the term originated, but salt pork was a long-lasting foodstuff used as a ration for armies and navies from the seventeenth century onwards. It would have been a staple food that could help keep a frontier family alive through the hard days of winter. The nineteenth-century American writer James Fennimore Cooper, best known for his novel *The Last of the Mohicans*, wrote in *The Chainbearer*, which is set during America's great expansion from the country's original European settlements on the East Coast into the mid- and far-western territories: "I hold a family to be in a desperate way, if the mother can see the bottom of the pork barrel."

To "see the bottom of the pork barrel" meant facing hunger and even starvation. Whatever the derivation of the term, pork-barrel politics came to mean the implementation of policies using national funding to deliver core benefits to politicians' local constituents. This only helped to ensure local favor for the politician through the sometimes inefficient allocation of national funds pleasing constituents. This in theory further encouraged citizens to vote for them again in the future. The term has become so accepted that people have shortened it to just "pork." The US nonprofit Citizens Against Government Waste (CAGW) follows the theme by publishing its annual *Congressional Pig Book Summary* to bring attention to the worst examples of pork spending, including nominating various lawmakers for its "Porkers of the Month" award.

Pork-barrel politics take us back to the mysterious case of $183 million of funding for tanks that the US Army had explicitly said it did not want. In 2012, the chair of the Subcommittee on Strategic Forces was Congressman Mike Turner, who represented the State of Ohio, home to the Lima Army Tank Plant. In December 2012, they assigned him an additional role as Chairman of the Tactical Air and Land Services Subcommittee, granting him oversight of further military spending programs. His state is also home to the Wright-Patterson Air Force Base in Dayton.

Turner, who in 2024 is still in Congress, is unabashed about the power these roles gave him to ensure funding for these military institutions. His government website boasted at the time of his new appointment:

> The new subcommittee leadership role makes Turner responsible for oversight of a broad portfolio of Army, Navy, Marine Corps and Air Force acquisition programs. This is key to such Ohio military facilities as Wright-Patterson Air Force Base, the Lima Tank Plant, as well as Army and Air National Guard Bases.
>
> "I'd like to thank Chairman McKeon for his leadership on the committee, and for appointing me to this new position. With looming defense cuts and the potential of another round of BRAC [the Base Realignment and Closure program designed to increase Department of Defense efficiency] in the coming years, this subcommittee places me in a role to continue my strong advocacy for the men and women at Wright-Patt, the Lima Tank Plant, and a number of other facilities which preserve the safety and security of our nation," said Turner.[2]

---

2   Office of Congressman Michael Turner, "Turner Appointed Chairman of the Tactical Air & Land Forces Subcommittee," press release, December 12, 2012, https://turner.house.gov/2012/12/turner-appointed-chairman-of-the-tactical-air-land-forces-subcommittee.

In 2014, Turner announced further upgrades to Abrams tanks—again in the face of continued resistance from the army. On this occasion, he said that Congress "recognizes the necessity of the Abrams tank to our national security and authorizes an additional $120 million for Abrams tank upgrades. This provision keeps the production lines open in Lima, Ohio, and ensures that our skilled, technical workers are protected."[3] An analyst for the Center for Strategic and Budgetary Assessments, Todd Harrison, commented that it was not uncommon for Congress to go against the recommendation of the military and act in what he called a "parochial" way. "It's just one example and it's not unique to this year…In some cases, Congress is using its appropriate role of oversight. In some cases, Congress can act out of purely parochial interests."[4]

In fiscal year 2021, the CAGW identified $16.8 billion of pork spending through what is known in the United States as "earmarks," which allocate specific funding within large spending bills to a particular local project. According to the *2021 Congressional Pig Book Summary*, the earmarks included a record $25 million for Save America's Treasures grants (56.3 percent greater than the $16 million in Fiscal

---

3 Richard Sisk, "Congress Again Buys Abrams Tanks the Army Doesn't Want," Military.com, December 18, 2014, https://www.military.com/daily-news/2014/12/18/congress-again-buys-abrams-tanks-the-army-doesnt-want.html.
4 Sisk, "Congress Again Buys."

Year 2020) and $1.7 billion for seventeen unrequested F-35 Joint Strike Fighter (JSF) aircraft. This aircraft has been plagued with cost overruns, delays, and poor performance. In the past, they have funded the restoration and operation of local museums, opera houses, and theatres; a record $19.7 million for the East-West Center, which was added by Senate Appropriations Committee member Brian Schatz (D-Hawaii), even though there was no budget request; and, $663,000 to help eliminate the brown tree snake.

The East-West Center aimed to strengthen relations among the peoples of Asia, the Pacific, and the US, while the brown tree snake was a problem in Guam, a small US island territory in the western Pacific.

To qualify as pork, policies listed in the *Congressional Pig Book* must meet one of seven criteria: "Requested by only one chamber of Congress; Not specifically authorized; Not competitively awarded; Not requested by the President; Greatly exceeds the President's budget request or the previous year's funding; Not the subject of congressional hearings; or, Serves only a local or special interest."[5]

Lobbyists can use earmarks within spending bills to "buy" lawmakers' votes by persuading a politician who opposes a

---

5   Sean Kennedy, *2021 Congressional Pig Book Summary*, ed. Thomas A. Schatz (Washington, DC: Citizens against Government Waste, 2022), 7, https://www.cagw.org/sites/default/files/pdf/2021PigBook.pdf.

particular bill to support it in exchange for money being earmarked for a popular project in their home constituency. A moratorium on earmarks declared in 2012 did not stop the practice, as Congress coined a new term for continued congressionally directed spending: "community project funding." CAGW noted these earmarks in appropriation bills, and though they fell after the 2012 moratorium to an average of 109 projects costing $3.7 billion annually between fiscal years 2012 and 2017, they quickly rebounded to an average of 268 projects costing $15.7 billion annually for the period 2018 to 2021.[6] Congress announced it would end the moratorium on earmarks in 2021.[7]

Alaska's "Bridge to Nowhere" was a final example of a spectacularly obvious piece of pork that seems to have contributed to the 2012 moratorium on earmarks. In 2005, $223 million of funding was earmarked within a large federal highway transportation bill to fund the building of a bridge connecting the Alaska town of Ketchikan (population of less than nine thousand) to an airport on Gravina Island (population of around fifty), which is separated from Ketchikan by a narrow strait of water. Later, the earmarks were rescinded, and Reuters

---

6 Kennedy, *Congressional Pig Book*, 2.
7 Jennifer Shutt, "House Appropriators Officially Bring Back Earmarks, Ending Ban," *Roll Call*, February 26, 2021, https://rollcall.com/2021/02/26/house-appropriators-to-cap-earmarks-at-1-percent-of-topline/.

reported that an Alaska Department of Transportation spokesperson said, "There is a lower-cost alternative using existing assets."[8] This alternative was upgrades to existing ferry services, which took fifteen minutes to connect the airport with Ketchikan. By the time the project was scrapped, the proposed "Bridge to Nowhere" had seen projected costs rise to above $400 million.[9]

MODELING PORK-BARREL SPENDING

Because representative politicians have built-in incentives to indulge in "pork-barrel politics," economists widely believe that all legislatures based on geographic representation will always be tempted to implement such inefficient policies. In an article titled "Inefficiency in Legislative Policymaking: A Dynamic Analysis" published in 2007 in *The American Economic Review*, Marco Battaglini of Princeton University and Stephen Coate of Cornell University reported that "[a]ccording to conventional wisdom, legislators will try to benefit their constituents at the expense of the general community through pork-barrel spending and other distributive policies."[10]

---

8   Steve Quinn, "Alaska's 'Bridge to Nowhere' Plan Finally Scrapped," Reuters, October 23, 2015, https://www.reuters.com/article/world/us/alaskas-bridge-to-nowhere-plan-finally-scrapped-idUSKCN0SI000/.
9   Quinn, "Alaska's 'Bridge to Nowhere' Plan."
10 Marco Battaglini and Stephen Coate, "Inefficiency in Legislative...

Battaglini and Coate set out to build a complex model of this legislative policymaking. They distinguished between "public goods"—spending on things that benefit all citizens, such as national defense and improved air quality—and "district-specific unproductive transfers (pork-barrel spending)." In their model, legislators would choose an appropriate level of taxation to raise revenues that were then spent in differing proportions on either public goods or pork.

Their model incorporates a system of dynamic political bargaining where a randomly selected legislator makes a proposal regarding the income tax rate and proposes new levels of public good and/or district-specific spending that affects only the residents of various districts. If a set number of other legislatures do not accept the theoretical proposal, they select another legislator to make a new proposal. If legislators cannot agree on any other proposed policies, they enact a default policy that treats every district uniformly. This means if transfers are made to any one district, they must be made to every other district as well. The model also considers that public goods accumulate a benefit funded in one round of legislation will continue to provide benefits to citizens in future legislative rounds,

---

...Policymaking: A Dynamic Analysis," *American Economic Review* 97, no. 1 (March 2007): 118–149, https://doi.org/10.1257/aer.97.1.118.

considering a factor for the depreciation rate of any public good and a measure of the relative importance of that public good to citizens.

Battaglini and Coate's mathematical model identifies various types of political equilibrium. It shows that when the stock of public good is low, legislators will not propose spending money on pork-barrel transfers because the only way to fund them is by reducing public investment or increasing taxation. The marginal benefit of public investment and the marginal cost of increased taxation are both too high. What the authors call the "collective utility" of all legislators is maximized by keeping taxation as low and public investment as high as possible, without any inefficient spending on pork-barrel policies.

However, once the stock of public good is sufficiently high, there is an incentive for legislators to include pork-barrel spending for their districts and also for the minimum number of other legislators' districts that will guarantee enough support for their proposal.

Battaglini and Coate identify a threshold level of public good. Below this, legislators will look for what they call a "unanimous coalition solution" for public investment funded by a minimum necessary level of taxation to gain the support of every legislator. Beyond that threshold, legislators will opt for a "minimum winning coalition solution" where they distribute enough benefits to districts other than their own to secure the necessary votes for their proposed policies to be accepted.[11]

It is a highly elegant mathematical model the authors argue provides a "rigorous formal underpinning" for the argument that political systems based on geographical representation (or other kinds of constituency) will cause political horse-trading that "leads to both excessive spending and a misallocation of government revenues between distributive policies and important national public goods."[12] The authors note that in economies where revenue from taxation is small compared to public needs, policy decisions will be efficient in the long term, even where legislators can benefit their districts via distributive policies (because legislators will not get majority support for such distribution policies). They also flag an unexpected corollary—that there is a risk that legislators in low-tax-revenue economies could hold back on public spending out of a concern that creating too much public good could lead future legislators to indulge in pork barrel, distributive policies. Otherwise, they are reliant on future legislators being what Battaglini and Coate call "virtuous" by responding to the reduced need to invest

---

11 Battaglini and Coate, "Inefficiency in Legislative Policymaking."
12 Battaglini and Coate, "Inefficiency in Legislative Policymaking," 118.

in public good by reducing taxes rather than by indulging in pork-barrel spending.[13]

Because they are economists, Battaglini, and Coate assume the legislators in their model will act in rational yet self-interested ways, doing whatever it takes to get the most "utility" for their constituency but constrained because greater utility may come from investment in public good rather than in distributive transfers. They do *not* assume their model legislators will corruptly divert public revenues to themselves and to people who can further their interests. Of course, many countries are plagued by this corruption.

In the next chapter, I will look at other reasons why humans have an inbuilt tendency to make bad policy decisions. The apparent inevitability of pork-barrel spending in any form of distributive policymaking, where politicians have good reasons to want to please their constituencies, is a powerful argument for taking such policymaking out of the hands of humans and giving it to machines.

Handing control of much of our policymaking to new systems would shortcut both the tendency of politicians to further their political careers by diverting national funds to their constituencies and the all-too-human tendency for outright corruption. It would also remove the need for current

---

13 Battaglini and Coate, "Inefficiency in Legislative Policymaking," 143.

legislators to worry about whether future legislators will be "virtuous"—reducing future taxation, for example, because of current sound policies and holding back public spending rather than indulging in pork-barrel spending, because machines do what we program them to do, while politicians are driven by their self-interest.

CHAPTER 3

THE CHALLENGE OF COMPLEXITY

THE LAST CHAPTER COVERED THE PRESSURES THAT exist for politicians to spend national funds inefficiently in any form of representative government to favor their political interests.

Another issue that challenges every human policymaker, no matter how "virtuous" they may be, is that of complexity. Many policies provide an ideal solution to a highly complex situation. But it is extremely difficult—if not hard—to predict how truly complex systems will behave. Policymakers are terrible at creating effective policies to address highly complex scenarios.

THE FIVE PATHOLOGIES OF COMPLEX SYSTEMS

In a 2020 paper in *EconomiA* entitled "Why Public Policies Fail: Policymaking under Complexity," Bernardo Mueller of the University of Brasilia, Brazil, identifies what he calls five "pathologies" of complex systems.[1]

NONLINEARITY IS HARD TO CHART

The first, argues Mueller, is that complex systems are nonlinear and emergent, whereas economic theory is linear. Economic theory assumes that demand in an economy is the sum of the demand of every individual within it. This assumption works well most of the time, but is constantly being upended by the vagaries of human behavior. Irrational "booms" and subsequent "busts" are classic examples: Holland's Tulip Mania in the early seventeenth century; Britain's South Sea bubble of 1720 (leading to the world's first financial crash); France's Mississippi Bubble of the same era; Railway Mania in Britain in the nineteenth century; the Wall Street Crash of 1929; the twenty-first century's dot-com bubble; and the US housing bubble that led to the Great Recession. These outbursts of what the former chair

---

[1] Bernardo Mueller, "Why Public Policies Fail: Policymaking under Complexity," *EconomiA* 21, no. 2 (May–August 2020): 311–323, https://doi.org/10.1016/j.econ.2019.11.002.

of the US Federal Reserve, Alan Greenspan, called "irrational exuberance" are impossible to predict—though it is usually possible to realize that a bubble is in progress once it has begun in earnest.

Complex systems are also susceptible to tipping points and discontinuities. Ecosystems and weather systems exemplify complex systems that may seem to withstand increasing amounts of change, but can suddenly transition into a different state without warning when they reach an unpredictable tipping point. One topical and alarming potential one relates to the ocean current called the Atlantic Meridional Overturning Circulation (AMOC). Warm water from the tropics flows northwards, losing water from evaporation and becoming saltier and cooling as it heads toward the Arctic. This cooler, denser ocean water is heavier, sinking deep into the ocean and then flowing back southwards. Eventually, as it warms, it rises again, creating a "conveyor belt" of warm water that keeps the northern hemisphere much warmer than it would otherwise be. But the melting of arctic ice and increased rainfall caused by global warming are diluting the warm, salty northward current, potentially preventing it from sinking and thereby destroying the "conveyor belt."

Historic evidence points to previous abrupt changes in the AMOC, suggesting the existence of a threshold that could tip the system to collapse. The UK's Meteorological Office predicts outcomes of a collapse of AMOC: "An AMOC shutdown would cause cooling of the northern hemisphere, sea level rise in the Atlantic, an overall decrease in precipitation over Europe and North America, and a southwards shift in monsoons in South America and Africa. These impacts are robust and seen in many models, but their magnitude remains uncertain."[2] Tipping points are real and have dramatic consequences that are hard to predict.

WE DON'T KNOW WHAT WE DON'T KNOW

Mueller's second pathology is a variation on his theme that "public policies do not settle into equilibria and [are] hard to predict." We assume we can know every future state of the world, whereas, of course, we cannot. Mueller makes the interesting point that, with highly complex systems, we may not even know what we need to predict: "you not only don't know what will happen, you don't know what *can* happen" [emphasis added].

---

[2] Met Office, *Risk Management of Climate Thresholds and Feedbacks: Atlantic Meridional Overturning Circulation (AMOC)* (London: The Meteorological Office, 2019), 1, https://www.metoffice.gov.uk/binaries/content/assets/metofficegovuk/pdf/weather/learn-about/climate/deliverables/amoc.pdf.

THINGS CHANGE

Mueller's third pathology follows his argument that the complex cultural, institutional, and technological environment in which public policies exist is constantly evolving, and policy must evolve to adapt to this—but that complex systems don't have a "single global maximum" that represents the "one knowable best choice." It is easy to settle for a local, decent solution, "even when there are better solutions nearby."

HUMANS AREN'T REALLY RATIONAL ANIMALS

Mueller's fourth pathology is a commonly accepted problem of cognitive bias: behavioral economics has shown convincingly that human beings do not behave according to the standard model of rational choice theory, so we must accept that well-intentioned and apparently rational policies may not have the expected effect.

PEOPLE ARE HARD TO FIGURE

Finally, Mueller highlights occasions when policies fail because the people impacted by the policy react in unexpected ways.

THE CHALLENGE OF MANAGING FISHERIES

As an example of policymaking in a complex public arena, Mueller uses the attempt to prevent the overfishing of world fisheries using the Individual Transferable Quotas (ITQs) for fishing rights. Overfishing is a classic example of "the tragedy of the commons"—a concept that gained traction after the publication of a now-famous 1968 essay with that title by the ecologist Garrett Hardin (the concept was first expounded in 1833 by the British economist William Forster Lloyd).

Hardin noted that if a group of herdsmen all graze their cattle on common land, then every herdsman can benefit by grazing extra cattle, and they all share the cost of the additional consumption of grass by more cattle. In Hardin's argument, any individual herdsman will note that the utility to him of grazing an extra animal is close to +1 and the effects of overgrazing are shared by all, making the negative utility a fraction of –1. As Hardin writes:

> The rational herdsman concludes that the only sensible course for him to pursue is to add another animal to his herd. And another; and another…But this is the conclusion reached by each and every rational herdsman sharing a commons. Therein is the tragedy. Each man is locked into a system that compels him to increase his herd without

limit—in a world that is limited. Ruin is the destination toward which all men rush, each pursuing his own best interest in a society that believes in the freedom of the commons. Freedom in a commons brings ruin to all.[3]

Hardin's essay addressed the apparently inevitable (and exponential) growth of the world's human population, which Hardin felt would inevitably lead to the exhaustion of the world's resources. The ability to feed the world's population remains a pressing concern, but we now see that, as individual populations become more affluent, they reduce the number of children they have: they do not follow Hardin's compelling logic that more children will bring more benefit and that if they do not produce as many children as possible, their neighbors will step into the void and use up resources to raise their own large families. The United Nations *World Population Prospects 2022* report forecasts that the world's population will peak at 10.43 billion in 2086 and then decline through 2100.[4]

It is also true that humans repeatedly show the ability to cooperate in order to avoid bad outcomes—to come together

---

3 Garrett Hardin, "The Tragedy of the Commons," *Science* 162, no. 3859 (1968): 1244, https://doi.org/10.1126/science.162.3859.1243.
4 United Nations Department of Economic and Social Affairs Population Division, *World Population Prospects 2022* (New York: United Nations, 2022), https://population.un.org/wpp/Download/Standard/MostUsed/.

and decide on various forms of restraint that will benefit the community. The "tragedy of the commons" may not be as inevitable as Hardin suggests. If a desirable resource is available to all comers and there is no social pressure or appetite for restraint, it is absolutely the case that the resource will be exploited until it is exhausted. Common fisheries—our shared oceans—offer a perfect example.

The classic economic solution to the tragedy of the commons is to avoid common ownership through introducing private property. In fisheries, the concept of ITQs introduces what Mueller describes as "property rights to fish and a market in which these rights can be traded."[5] Governments determine the sustainable level of extraction for each fishery and set the quotas accordingly. Holders of ITQs then use their rights to catch and land fish, or they can sell their rights on the market. This had the benefit that the most efficient fishermen—those who could catch fish at the lowest cost could buy quotas off other, less efficient fishermen.

The entire scheme has considerable economic elegance. Sadly, it doesn't seem to have worked. Mueller mentions a 2008 study that concluded that introducing some form of ITQs to 121 fisheries within a total database of over 11,000 fisheries had reduced the probability of a fisheries

---

5   Mueller, "Why Public Policies Fail," 313.

collapse by a factor of less than 14 percent—arguably better than nothing, but not a dramatic success. Another study of twenty fisheries using ITQs showed that only twelve had seen an improvement in fish stocks. A meta-study analyzed 227 papers evaluating the effect of ITQs and found that "23% reported negative effects on fish stocks and 14% mixed effects"—hardly the significant positive effect on fish stocks that was the aim of the policy.[6]

Daniel Bromley of the University of Wisconsin–Madison, in "Abdicating Responsibility: The Deceits of Fisheries Policy," published in *Fisheries Magazine*, stated that ITQs are "the natural resource equivalent of economic deregulation dating back to the triumphalism of the 1990s."[7] This was the era following the collapse of the Soviet Union when free market thinking was ascendant and it was believed by many economists that, as Bromley puts it, "government (the realm of collective action—'politics') must not be allowed to interfere with the economy (the realm of alleged individual 'freedom')."[8]

It is true that ITQs are often present as a self-sustaining mechanism where the invisible hand of the market will ensure rational, self-interested fishers are granted property rights

---

6   Mueller, "Why Public Policies Fail," 313–314.
7   Daniel W. Bromley, "Abdicating Responsibility: The Deceits of Fisheries Policy," *Fisheries Magazine* 34, no. 6 (June 2009): 281, https://doi.org/10.1577/1548-8446-34.6.280.
8   Bromley, "Abdicating Responsibility," 280.

over their quota of fish will ensure the sustainability of fishing stocks. In practice, owners of fishing quotas may be forced to "discard" (throw back into the water) fish they have caught because they have exceeded their quota, with the real risk that a high proportion of discarded fish will be damaged or already dead, "high grade" their catches (discarding less valuable fish in favor of higher-value fish species), or even indulge in straightforward quota busting. The prevention of these practices must be funded by national governments because ITQs are granted to the commercial fishing sector at no cost.

Bromley argues that the total allowable catch (TAC) set by governments based on the best assessments of sustainable catch levels is the only meaningful mechanism at play, and that the ITQs merely represent a "catch share" allocated to individual commercial fishing operations. "Science-based TACs—assiduously enforced," argues Bromley, "are the necessary and sufficient condition for sustainability in fisheries."[9] He also argues that, instead of free gifting fishing quotas to commercial fishing operations, those operations should submit bids for the royalty they are prepared to pay on their earnings to "the owners of the fish" (the people of the government concerned), thus giving the state a source of income to fund the essential policing of fisheries.

---

9   Bromley, "Abdicating Responsibility," 288.

Free marketeers praised the exquisitely elegant solution offered by ITQs, creating temporary private ownership of fish stock to allow the market to work its supposed magic. The results were mixed, and there remains a great deal of scope for fishing operations to game the system, requiring expensive management and policing. The solution, as Bromley suggests, may be far simpler:

If people are caught in the act of overfishing, penalties are imposed. Human societies, over a rather long history, have figured out how to prevent all manner of unwanted activities and outcomes—from child pornography to organized dog fighting. It is no great mystery, and ownership plays no part in the story. Only fisheries economists—and ideologues—believe that property rights (or the lack thereof) explain overfishing.[10]

Since Bromley has argued that the (simple) answer to achieving sustainability in fisheries is "science-based TACs—assiduously enforced," it is easy to imagine that a more sophisticated solution might be to plug all available global data about fish stocks and their sustainability into machines and allow them to determine—at the most local level the data will sustain—what is the level of TAC for any individual fishery. This would be followed by allocating shares to that TAC

---

10 Bromley, "Abdicating Responsibility," 281.

by whatever system is most efficient (such as royalty-based bids) and finally enforce that rigorously, using funds generated by the fishing companies that are being granted access to this precious shared resource.

Another complex area of policymaking is the use of tariffs to regulate trade between nation-states. One of the obvious perils (and benefits) of globalization is that one country could produce certain goods at a competitive price and that the import of these cheaper goods into other countries undermines domestic industries, leading to shuttered factories and lost jobs. Sometimes countries subsidize the production of some manufactured goods and may then "dump" these goods at unreasonably low prices in other countries—perhaps to gain market share, perhaps simply to shift inventory, or perhaps for more insidious political reasons. Politicians, not surprisingly, respond to low-cost imports by imposing tariffs to level the playing field and protect domestic industries from such, arguably unfair, competition.

Industries such as steel manufacturing are often the beneficiaries of import tariffs because nation-states can manufacture their own steel—if a nation finds itself at war, for example, it is reassuring to build tanks and ships and armaments from its own steel rather than relying on imports that may be blocked by newly hostile foreign suppliers. Steel manufacturing infrastructure, once lost, is also hard to resurrect at short notice. Sometimes the reason for protecting a particular industry is more political: manufacturing industries are a significant and highly visible source of well-paid jobs. It is very difficult for politicians to stand by while an indigenous manufacturing industry is being hit hard by low-cost overseas imports.

In 2018, US President Donald Trump used his executive powers to impose increased tariffs on imports from China of steel, aluminum, and finished goods (including washing machines, solar panels, and a broad range of other products). Playing to his nativist base, Trump argued China was "laughing" at the United States. In a 2016 interview with the cable network Fox News, before tariffs were imposed, Trump stated, "I know many of the people in China, I know many of the big business people, and they're laughing at us. They think we're so stupid."[11] Trump often focused on the very real issue of intellectual property theft, including in his book *Time to Get Tough: Making America #1 Again*: "The Chinese laugh at how weak and pathetic our government is in combating intellectual property theft."[12]

---

11 Niraj Chokshi, "The 100-Plus Times Donald Trump Assured Us That America Is a Laughingstock," *The Washington Post*, January 27, 2016, https://www.washingtonpost.com/news/the-fix/wp/2016/01/27/the-100-plus-times-donald-trump-has-assured-us-the-united-states-is-a-laughingstock/.

12 Donald J. Trump, *Time to Get Tough: Making America #1 Again* (Washington, DC: Regnery Publishing, 2011), 42.

The *Washington Post* included many of these comments in an article entitled "The 100-Plus Times Donald Trump Assured Us That America Is a Laughingstock" as part of laying the political groundwork for imposing tariffs—on China in particular.[13] This emotional appeal to Trump's political base, suggesting that competitors were "laughing at" the United States because of its "weak" stance on imports and China's theft of US intellectual property strongly suggests that Trump's motivation for imposing the tariffs was political rather than economic. People who feel that increasing globalization is taking away well-paid jobs at home and damaging their standard of living can easily be persuaded that the correct policy is to impose tariffs on imports from foreign countries, which appears "strong" and straightforward.

As with all attempts to change complex systems, it's not as simple as that.

Tariffs are a tax designed to make imported goods more expensive and to reduce any "unfair" price advantage that imported goods might have. In 2019, the United States raised $79 billion from the newly imposed tariffs. Unfortunately, according to the American research group the Brookings Institution, American consumers ended up paying the bulk

---

13 Chokshi, "The 100-Plus Times."

of this $79 billion, rather than the foreign exporters of the goods concerned.

> The Trump administration has repeatedly argued that foreign companies are paying for tariffs. But multiple studies suggest this is not the case: the cost of tariffs have been borne almost entirely by American households and American firms, not foreign exporters. While estimates vary, economic analyses suggest the average American household has paid somewhere from several hundred up to a thousand dollars or more per year thanks to higher consumer prices attributable to the tariffs.[14]

The problem is that making imported Chinese steel more expensive in America may help the US steel industry—Brookings reported the creation of "several thousand jobs in the steel industry"—but it also impacts a far larger number of US companies that used imported Chinese steel to manufacture a huge range of products, and who were forced to increase prices of finished goods to compensate for the more expensive raw material.

---

14 Geoffrey Gertz, "Did Trump's Tariffs Benefit American Workers and National Security?," Brookings, September 10, 2020, https://www.brookings.edu/articles/did-trumps-tariffs-benefit-american-workers-and-national-security/.

In 2018, an economist reported in the *New York Times* that an estimated "140,000 American workers make steel, while 6.5 million workers make products that include steel." The result, according to the *Times* article, is that "the new tariffs hit many of the consumer products that Americans use every day" and that "the bill for this method of protecting domestic jobs [tariffs] is paid disproportionately by lower-income families." [15] Introducing tariffs is often justified as a way to protect domestic jobs, but it is a highly inefficient way of achieving this aim.

In 2009, US President Barack Obama imposed a tariff on the import of tires from China to protect jobs in the US tire manufacturing industry. The same *Times* article estimates that, at most, 1,200 jobs were saved—but that Americans paid an additional $1.1 billion for tires compared to pre-tariff price levels, meaning that each job saved in the US tire manufacturing industry had been "bought" at a cost of around $1 million—while the average annual wage for such a job was around $40,000.

The *Times* article concluded with some quotes from an interview with Paul Reitz, the CEO of Titan International, a US

---

15 Binyamin Appelbaum, "Trump Says Tariffs Will Save American Factories. History Shows Otherwise," *The New York Times*, September 17, 2018, https://www.nytimes.com/2018/09/17/us/politics/trump-tariffs-american-factories.html.

manufacturer of tires for farming equipment. Reitz was happy with the new tariffs on imports of tires from China because it allowed him to increase US prices for his company's products, earn higher profits, and use these for investment instead of "giving [profits] away to fight foreign competitors." But he was less keen on the tariffs on steel, which his company used to reinforce tires and manufacture wheels. A looming trade war with China was also impacting farmers—the tire manufacturer's core customer base—because China was retaliating by imposing its own tariffs on imports of US soy and pork. "It created a lot of uncertainty with our cost structure and our customers," Reitz told the *Times*. "We just don't know what the full impact of the tariffs are going to be."[16]

COMPLEXITY IN POLICYMAKING

Policymaking in highly complex areas of national and international affairs can have many unintended consequences. It rarely has the simple effect that the policymakers hope; it sometimes has bad and even catastrophic side effects. Machine intelligence is very good at complexity—at analyzing very large numbers of scenarios to choose the most effective route to a desired outcome. Machines can now

---

16 Appelbaum, "Trump Says Tariffs."

routinely defeat human masters of chess and the more complex ancient Chinese game of Go—and can even teach themselves how to do this with relatively little input from human beings once a self-learning program is put into place (as covered in a coming chapter). Machines can make better decisions than human beings in complex arenas where there is a very large number of possible different outcomes arising from any one change to the current system. As we will see, there are an estimated 10^{120} game variations in chess and 2×10^{170} variations in the game of Go—and machines now outperform humans in both.[17] Our fond belief in human "intuition" has been a delusion—and, in the case of Go, machines are finding new strategies that at first confound, and then greatly impress, the most brilliant human players. It seems there may be better, more effective strategies for the game of Go that humans have not been able to devise.

Machines are also terrific at offering solutions for "multi-agent" problems where there are many competing interests, and the challenge is to find the one outcome that represents the best compromise for everyone involved—exactly the problem posed by international trade agreements and other multinational negotiations.

---

17   Michael Kanaan, *T-Minus AI: Humanity's Countdown to Artificial Intelligence and the New Pursuit of Global Power* (Dallas, TX: BenBella Books, 2020), loc. 1566, Kindle.

I spoke to Lauri Almann, co-founder of BHC Laboratory, an Estonian cybersecurity company about complexity in policymaking and the apparent impossibility of knowing that policies put in place in complex situations will have the desired effect. Almann advises the Estonian government and has served in various top-level civil service positions there, including as permanent secretary of the Ministry of Defense and on the team that organized the response to cyberattacks against Estonia in 2007. Almann told me:

> Our problem, basically, is that our decision-making is almost always reactive. We call it strategic decision-making in governance, but it's not. It's not actually taking strategic decisions; it is in fact reacting to stuff happening right now. When we create scenarios for our decision-makers, we are playing with the world as it is—the world that we use to model the future of decision-making is actually the world that we know. But the future world will not be like that.

He argues that to help leaders plan for what the future will look like, as opposed to the future that we instinctively predict based on our current experiences, we need to consider many—possibly radically different—futures.

His consultancy has contributed to several high-level, future-scenario-planning sessions involving EU ministers of defense and internal affairs. To cope with the inherent unpredictability of complex systems, Almann's consultancy has introduced the concept of multiple futures—imagined futures in which "the world as we know it now has changed in some fundamental way." As an example, he thinks back to a cybersecurity conference he attended in 2006, one year before Apple introduced the iPhone. There were mobile phones with some level of internet connection, but the iPhone would allow users to browse the internet exactly as they would on their desktops and laptops. The explosion of various smartphone technologies that quickly followed changed everything.

A world in which nearly everyone carries with them a powerful computer with full internet access, GPS tracking, and a high-quality onboard camera has transformed the world in a number of ways that were—often literally—unthinkable beforehand.

"The Symantec cybersecurity forecast in 2006 completely ignored smartphones," Almann points out, "and because they didn't imagine that future, their forecasts about how the world would look just a few years later were completely wrong."

Another example Almann offers is how the COVID-19 pandemic caught the world by surprise—even though, as he told me, he clearly remembers reading a 1998 book showing that, based on previous history, the world was overdue for a major new pandemic of some kind. Nation after nation discovered painfully that they did not, in fact, have "ready-to-roll" policies in place at the onset of COVID-19. Researchers developed successful vaccines against the new virus astonishingly quickly. The mechanics of mass track-and-trace and vaccination programs and/or population lockdowns aimed at slowing the spread of the disease had to be invented by the world's nations more or less from scratch. The use of machine intelligence to imagine multiple futures and devise policies that would help us cope with new and unexpected scenarios could provide us with a set of policy toolkits that could be taken "off the shelf" and quickly implemented.

To help with planning for unpredictable futures, Almann suggests the creation of "scenario backbones"—a set of key issues that are of most concern—and then running models of how those scenario backbones would be impacted in a range of radically different futures. He explains:

> The idea of multiple futures—decision-making based on multiple futures—means that we don't know what the future might be. But in our decision-making, we should be able to identify an event that is critical to us and see how it starts relating to other events around us. And there is a lot of data involved. There are lots of alternatives involved. We could learn from those future looks so much.

Coping with the pandemic itself—or any other future shock—was not the only problem faced by policymakers. Many pre-pandemic forecasts and policies based on the world as it was before the pandemic have had to be torn up as inflation, tax revenues, and public expenditures have changed dramatically from previous estimates. Likewise, the pandemic has disrupted healthcare systems. The total impact of the social disruption caused by the pandemic is still difficult to assess.

A 2021 article published in *Frontiers in Public Health* observed that pre-modern pandemics caused "serious demographic shifts, mortality shocks, and social and political disturbance."[18] The Black Death, for example, caused so many deaths in medieval Europe that there was a shortage of labor, and wages were forced to rise. The aristocracy attempted to force wages back to pre-plague levels by legislation, leading to social unrest and, eventually, to the end of the feudal system. We have yet to see what kind of disturbances the COVID-19 pandemic will lead to in modern society. Running scenario backbones against futures like Almann does—including an imagined post-pandemic future—would have made us far better prepared for the reality we now face.

---

18   Yunfeng Shang, Haiwei Li, and Ren Zhang, "Effects of Pandemic Outbreak on Economies: Evidence from Business History Context," *Frontiers in Public Health* 9, no. 632043 (March 2021), https://doi.org/10.3389/fpubh.2021.632043.

The increasing availability of a vast amount of data about our current behaviors suggests that machines will be better positioned than humans to run models of possible futures and predict various outcomes. This is because humans find it challenging to imagine worlds that are significantly different from their own. Machines don't suffer from the human bias of "creeping determinism" (the assumption that inevitable things would turn out how they have) and will happily consider a future very different from the past.

I would like to introduce one final thought to this commentary regarding the weaknesses and foibles of human policymakers. Politicians, after implementing a failed policy, have good reason to not admit that it has failed and repeal the policy. As a result, many failed policies remain on the statute books. A 2001 article by Robert A. J. Dur of the Erasmus University, Rotterdam, uses game theory to prove that "if the policy maker cares sufficiently about holding office, he will never repeal a policy, even if the policy does more harm than good."[19]

Dur argues that voters lack perfect knowledge of the effects of the implemented policy. If voters knew for certain that a policy had failed, then an admission by a politician that it had indeed failed—and should be repealed—would not be

---

19 Robert A. J. Dur, "Why Do Policy Makers Stick to Inefficient Decisions?," *Public Choice* 107, no. 3/4 (June 2001): 221, https://doi.org/10.1023/A:1010305204751.

new information influencing their decision to vote for the politician (or not) at election time. But voters, most times, have imperfect knowledge of the real-world outcomes of policies.

Larger trends and outside forces that are beyond any politicians' control influence many policies. So, voters can never be certain if a policy has failed because it was badly conceived or because events have overtaken it. Dur gives as examples attempts to reduce unemployment or stimulate economic growth—macroeconomic goals that even well-designed policies may fail to achieve because of events beyond policymakers' control.

In other cases, maybe a policy affects only a small proportion of voters, so that most people are unaware of whether the policy has been a success or not. Changes to taxation or benefits that affect only a small number of people would be an example.

Dur's last example is a policy that only takes effect in certain circumstances or after a subsequent election. Long-term investments or defense spending would be good examples: by the time long-term investments are shown to have worked, voters are likely to have forgotten who handled them; defense spending may seem adequate until some new threat proves otherwise.

Dur's compelling argument is that admitting that a particular policy has been a failure reflects badly on a politician's competence, and that it is often the case that the voting public is only partially aware of any policy's success or failure. So, it is always in a politician's interests to stick with a failed policy rather than face the possible electoral consequences of admitting failure.[20]

An example of politicians' unwillingness to admit to policy failure is the UK's infamous "poll tax" (launched as the Community Charge) imposed by Prime Minister Margaret Thatcher in Scotland, England, and Wales in the late 1980s and early 1990s. Taxes for local government had been raised by a system of "rates" payable by property owners and tenants. There was an argument that the new tax would be fairer because, for example, a widowed pensioner living alone paid the same amount in rates as a family of five or six people living in one house, several of whom might be wage earners, and all of whom would use local government services. Every adult would pay the poll tax, in contrast, at a level set by the UK's local authorities. A large part of Conservative Prime Minister Thatcher's political logic had been that non-rates-paying citizens (those who were not householders) had an incentive to vote for left-leaning councils that offered high levels of local government services and benefits but who did not have to shoulder the burden of the higher local tax rates that went

---

20 Dur, "Why Do Policy Makers," 221–234.

along with high-spending plans. If everyone had to pay their share of local taxes, it was thought they would tend to vote for lower-spending (typically conservative) local politicians. It was also believed that making every resident in local councils a fee-paying "customer" would encourage residents to hold councils responsible for the level of service provided and make councils more accountable to their "customers."

But the key problem with the poll tax was that the public perceived it to be a flat-rate tax and inherently unfair: the upper- or middle-class owners of expensive houses, who had funded a substantial proportion of local government spending the previous system of rates, saw their level of local taxation fall significantly, while many less-well-off citizens found themselves paying a significant new tax. The tax was also difficult to collect, as it required registering very large numbers of individual citizens. Rates had been collected from some fourteen million households; the poll tax required tax officials to track and collect taxes from some thirty-eight million adults.

The derogatory term "poll tax" quickly replaced the official term, "Community Charge," in popular usage because the tax bore a distinct similarity to a medieval "poll tax" introduced in England in the fourteenth century to finance the Hundred Years' War with France. That earlier tax was imposed on every man and woman over the age of fourteen "with the exception of honest beggars."[21] It was later revised to take into account rank and social position, but it was seen as fundamentally unfair because it failed to take account of citizens' ability to pay. Hostility to it was one factor leading up to the Peasants' Revolt of 1381, triggered when a royal official attempted to collect unpaid poll taxes in the county of Essex, which led to violent unrest that quickly spread across the region and resulted in an attack on the capital, London.

Nations have long memories. The twentieth century's poll tax led to riots where hundreds of people and police officers were injured and to a widespread campaign of non-registration and nonpayment. Britain's opposition left-wing Labour Party benefited, though it chose to oppose the law-breaking nonpayment campaign. "Law makers must not be law breakers," said Neil Kinnock, then leader of the Labour Party.[22] But Prime Minister Thatcher refused to repeal her flagship tax policy—confirming Dur's thesis that politicians will rarely confess to policy failure—and was toppled soon afterward as leader of the Conservative Party. She was replaced by John Major, who abolished the poll tax in his subsequent term of

---

21 "Tax Grant Details [poll tax, c. 1377 Feb 16 x 19]," The National Archives, accessed April 23, 2024, https://www.nationalarchives.gov.uk/e179/notes.asp?slctgrantid=403&action=3.

22 "1991: Anti-Poll Tax MP Jailed," BBC: On This Day, accessed April 23, 2024, http://news.bbc.co.uk/onthisday/hi/dates/stories/july/11/newsid_2500000/2500365.stm.

office after narrowly defeating a resurgent Labour Party in a general election. Major replaced the poll tax with a "Council Tax" based on property values whereby owners or renters of higher-value properties paid higher rates of local taxes. The Council Tax was remarkably similar to the system replaced by the ill-fated Community Charge.

INSIGHTS ACROSS BUREAUCRACIES

Policies need to be fair, efficient, and effective—and to be seen to be so. Policymaking in areas of real complexity is very likely to fail or have unintended effects, largely because it is based on the fundamental assumption that the future will be essentially similar to the world we are currently experiencing. But the policies introduced can have a radical effect on that future, changing "the world as we know it" and leading to unforeseen consequences.

Another expert I spoke to is Dr. Mark Powell, a partner at EY (formerly Ernst & Young) in London, head of the consultancy's data analytics practice. One of his clients is the British government:

> The insight-driven government would be radically driven from the policy-driven government which we have at the moment. Policymakers look at the available

information, which is usually relatively shallow and not data-driven—very often it's simply a report written by a civil servant based on the information that he or she has been able to pull together—and they come up with a new policy. That policy is effectively based on previous policy. The previous policy didn't work, or we are seeing some unintended consequence of the previous policy, so we introduce a new variation on that policy. What doesn't happen is that we interrogate all of the available data and look for new insights.

It is also currently true that much of the data that is theoretically available to governments is effectively siloed in different departments. There are also real privacy issues involved in pulling together all of the data governments have on individuals into a single database. But the huge benefits of interrogating significant amounts of anonymized data about people's social behaviors and their interactions with government will rapidly lead to socially acceptable access to large-scale data. This will lead to insightful, data-driven policymaking informed by real behaviors and fact-based evidence as to which government actions would most effectively bring about the desired outcomes. Dr. Powell sums up the future of insight-driven government as "data, data and more data, and the increasing use of artificial intelligence to gain insights from these millions upon millions of data points."

In the future, policymakers will forge policies based on data-driven insight and utilize machine intelligence to determine which government interventions are most likely to have the desired effect, while considering the various potential futures that may arise from the current world. This is, in an entirely literal sense, a "superhuman" task. It is best performed by machines able to deal with the volume of data involved and the complexities of the many outcomes that any individual course of action may unleash—and which are not influenced by the perverse or corrupt incentives human politicians face. It may seem hard to imagine we will ever give control of an essentially human activity—policymaking—to machines. But history shows that significant technological progress has always been accompanied by the growing automation, where machines gradually take control of functions that were initially performed by humans.

CHAPTER 4

LETTING MACHINES TAKE CONTROL

THE MARCH OF HUMAN PROGRESS IS PERHAPS BEST defined by our use of tools. We marvel when other species make even rudimentary use of tools: primates using stones to break crabs' shells to get at the meat inside or crows using sticks to get insects out of tree bark. We marvel because, for a time, we imagined we were the only tool-using species—and because it is clear how significant the use of tools has been in human development. We used to define epochs of human development by the primary materials used to make tools: the Stone Age, the Bronze Age, the Iron Age. Now we define our rapidly accelerating development by the technologies that drive each new phase of dramatic innovation: The First Industrial Revolution (steam power, machine tools, factories), the Second Industrial Revolution (scientific progress, mass production, industrialization), the Third Industrial Revolution (digital electronics computing, communications), and the Fourth Industrial Revolution (artificial intelligence, robotics, gene manipulation, nanotechnologies).

The more sophisticated our machines and technologies become, the more we turn to other machines and devices to allow those machines to reach their full capabilities. We realize that, if we control the machines ourselves, our human abilities will prevent the machines from demonstrating their full potential—realizing that, to a lesser or greater extent, we have to let machines take control.

THIS HAPPENED BEFORE COMPUTERS

The First Industrial Revolution, which began in Great Britain in the late eighteenth century, was one of the most transformational events in human history, ushering in an era of unprecedented economic growth and a steady improvement in the general standard of living. It allowed populations to grow while per capita income simultaneously rose. At the core of the Industrial Revolution was the now simple steam engine, with its ability to convert heat into mechanical work, offering an untapped power source to supplement humans' earlier dependence on the power of wind, water, and animals (including humans). And at the heart of the steam engine was a small and simple device that would allow the bigger machine to operate at maximum efficiency without human supervision: the centrifugal governor.

As the load on steam engines increased or decreased, it was necessary to adjust the flow of steam into the engine's cylinders to keep it operating at maximum efficiency. Too much load, and the engine would literally "run out of steam," failing to maintain the output. With a low load and plenty of steam, the engine would "run away," operating at faster and faster speeds to no effect. The ingenious solution was the centrifugal governor—two weighted balls attached to a central shaft by a sliding collar. As the shaft rotates faster, the centrifugal force on the spinning balls causes them to rise and a mechanical link translates this upward motion into a closing down of the fuel supply. More speed means less fuel; less speed means more fuel. The engine maintains a constant speed range without requiring a human to adjust the fuel supply in response to the varying loads. The machine has taken control of itself. By the way, modern turbines still utilize centrifugal governors.

From the moment we relied on machines to do work for us, we also thought about ways of getting machines to look after themselves. The centrifugal governor is associated with James Watt, whose improvements to the design of early steam engines are one of the main driving forces of the Industrial Revolution. Watt's key improvement to early steam engines included the introduction of the centrifugal governor, which controlled the speed at which the engines operated. However, it is important to note that the centrifugal governor had actually been invented in the previous century by the Dutch scientist and inventor Christiaan Huygens. Huygens designed it to regulate the distance and pressure between millstones in an earlier essential and equally revolutionary machine: the windmill. Different technology; the same impulse to allow the machines to control themselves.

The steam engine ruled for a century. Steam engines powered railway trains and ships, but by the time viable steam-powered cars for driving on roads were becoming workable, the internal combustion engine was gaining ascendancy. Steam engines were bulky and required constant attention. By around 1900, though, engineers had developed compact steam engines that could power an automobile and largely automated the process of supplying fuel and feedwater to the boiler. This partially solved the problem of the time taken to get a steam engine heated to operating temperature with "flash boilers" that heated small quantities of water at a time.

There was great alarm at the potential introduction of these steam-powered locomotives to the roads, which had always been the domain of pedestrians, horse riders, horse-drawn carriages, and farmers driving livestock from field to field or to market. There was real concern that the new "self-propelled" monsters would cause mayhem. In 1865, the Locomotive Act became law in the United Kingdom, requiring that a person walk in front of any self-propelled vehicle...

> ...and shall carry a red flag constantly, and shall warn the riders and drivers of horses of the approach of such locomotives, and shall signal the driver thereof when it shall be necessary to stop, and shall assist horses, and carriages drawn by horses, passing the same.

They repealed the law the next year. A similar law was introduced in the state of Vermont in the United States, requiring the "owner or person in charge of a carriage, vehicle or engine propelled by steam, except road rollers" to have a person walk one-eighth of a mile ahead of the vehicle to warn farmers with livestock of its approach.[1] That law was

---

[1] O. M. Barber, L. M. Read, and John Young, *The Vermont Statutes, 1894: Including the Public Acts of 1894, with the Declaration of Independence, the Articles of Confederation, and the Constitutions of the United States and the State of Vermont* (Rutland, VT: The Tuttle Company, 1895), 634.

repealed after two years.[2] People's concerns about "self-propelled vehicles" on public roads diminished as they realized the new locomotives were not uncontrollable juggernauts. They could be brought to a halt successfully by their drivers if a herd of sheep or cattle blocked the road ahead.

The world's first driverless vehicle, the operator-less elevator, received much less public acceptance. In the mid-nineteenth century, a New York factory manager called Elisha Graves Otis developed the world's first "safety elevator." Hoisting platforms of various kinds to lift goods to higher stories were in widespread use in factories, and they were notoriously unsafe. Otis's invention used a spring device to prevent the elevator platform from falling if the main hoisting rope or cable broke. He was able to demonstrate his safety elevator at the 1854 New York City Crystal Palace Exhibition of Industry of All Nations (considered the first world's fair in the US); a platform was hoisted high up above the crowds with Otis standing on it. A colleague dramatically severed the rope lifting the platform…and the platform fell just a few inches before coming to a stop. "All safe, gentlemen," cried Otis to the enthralled crowd. "All safe!"[3]

---

2   P. Aarne Vesilind and Thomas D. DiStefano, *Controlling Environmental Pollution: An Introduction to the Technologies, History, and Ethics* (Lancaster, PA: DEStech Publications, 2006), 400.
3   Wendy Ross, "The Rise—but Rarely the Fall—of the Elevator," *The Washington Post*, March 20, 1995, https://www.washingtonpost.com/archive/1995/03/21/…

The invention of the safety elevator coincided with the development of the steel-framed building, which ushered in the age of high-rise buildings. In 1857, Otis installed the world's first passenger elevator at the E. V. Haughwout Building—a fashionable glass, china, and silverware emporium in the SoHo neighborhood of Manhattan. A steam engine powered the elevator in the building's basement. Sadly, the building's management removed the elevator after only three years because most shoppers refused to use it.[4] But the increasing height of buildings made the elevator a necessity rather than a novelty. By the 1870s, elevators were being installed in New York office buildings. The elevator and the new "skyscrapers" of New York and Chicago were transforming the skyline and modern city life.

Operators ran all early elevators—elevator attendants. Bringing the elevator to a halt level with each floor of the building required skill. The operators also had to open and close doors, take the elevator to the required destination, and assist passengers entering and leaving. In department stores, elevator operators became part of the sales operation, announcing the goods available on each floor and advising shoppers where

---

...the-rise-but-rarely-the-fall-of-the-elevator/e4adcb4e-0e16-4dc4-9c78-a2739b4dd03b.

[4] Jacopo Prisco, "A Short History of the Elevator," CNN Style, February 9, 2019, https://www.cnn.com/style/article/short-history-of-the-elevator/index.html.

to find what they were looking for. In apartment buildings and office blocks, elevator attendants were a familiar, friendly, and helpful presence—a reassuring human touch.

As ever, engineers soon added various elements to elevators to improve safety and performance. One of these elements was the "self-levelling" elevator, which could align itself perfectly with the floor of each story. The industry introduced electric elevators in the late 1880s, and by 1900, it had developed completely automated elevators that required no human operator. However, the public was not prepared to use them. The consensus was that elevators—like trains, automobiles, and planes—needed human operators.

It took a strike of elevator operators, doormen, porters, and maintenance workers in New York City in 1945 to change public opinion. The strike brought the city to a halt and cost it an estimated $100 million in lost economic activity. Operating an elevator was not considered something an ordinary citizen should attempt. It was like driving a train or flying a passenger plane without the training and skills. Office workers climbed the countless flights of stairs in buildings, like the Empire State Building, to get to their offices.[5]

---

5   Henry Lawson Greenidge, "How A Historic Strike Paved the Way for the Automated Elevator and What Those Lessons Could Mean for Self-Driving Cars," Medium, May 12, 2020, https://henrylgreenidge.medium.com/how-a-historic-strike-paved-the-way-for-the-automated-elevator-and-what-those-lessons-could-mean-a0ae49993796.

But the strike changed public attitudes. Americans, self-reliant as ever, felt that maybe they should be able to operate an elevator themselves. Engineers gradually introduced automated elevators, equipping them with reassuring features like an emergency stop button and an emergency phone for passengers to call for help if anything went wrong. In 1950, Otis installed an automated elevator in the Atlantic Refining Building in Dallas, Texas. The unthinkable idea of using an elevator without an operator was about to become a routine part of modern life.

In the period between early alarm at the idea of "self-propelled" steam-powered cars on the roads of the United Kingdom and America, and the eventual acceptance of the self-operated elevator, the internal combustion engine had established itself as the power source of choice for most forms of transport. The only significant exception was electric trams and trains, which were introduced in the late nineteenth century.

The internal combustion engine was also completely dependent on mechanical feedback and automated control, with a cam-driven system opening an intake valve to draw in fuel at the beginning of a working stroke and opening an exhaust valve to remove combustion gases at the end. Engine management systems and safety features have increased in complexity ever since and become even more reliant on electronics. Today, automatic emergency braking systems, which use sensors to detect obstacles and apply the brakes if the driver fails to take action, look to become as standard as seat belts.

The self-driving car is, of course, the logical culmination of this process, and it will soon become as noncontroversial as using an elevator that has no operator. The growing use of automated forms of transport, and the increasing interconnectedness of a wide range of public facilities and common resources, will enable the automation of entire sections of public governance that previously relied on regulations, fines, taxes, incentives, and all the other paraphernalia of policymaking and government. What was once the domain of human planners and policymakers will become the domain of machines—either programmed to deliver key desired objectives or left to decide for themselves what the optimal objectives should even be under a set of overarching general principles that reflect human interests and key priorities.

But I am getting ahead of myself.

Before moving on, I should take the exploration of automation in transport to the next obvious level—from the development of the automobile to the early days of aviation and the almost immediate introduction of automation to the astonishing new flying machines. A mere nine years after the Wright brothers carried out the world's first flight of a powered, heavier-than-air machine at Kitty Hawk, North Carolina, their fellow American, Lawrence Sperry, invented the autopilot.

Sperry was just four days away from his eleventh birthday when the Wright brothers made their historic flight on December 17, 1903. He became entranced by the whole idea of human flight. In 1909, the teenager visited an air show at Mineola, Long Island, and made detailed notes about the designs of the early planes on display. He and his brother built their own glider in the family's basement summer house in Bellport, Long Island. When they realized they could not get the aircraft's wings out of the house, they removed the large, handsome bay windows from the front of the house to get them out into the garden where they assembled the aircraft. The boys' father did not find it amusing.

Sperry carried out a successful flight of the homemade aircraft, though with a slightly rough landing. He and his brother added a five-cylinder radial Anzani engine to the craft—the engine that had powered Louis Bleriot's first-ever flight across the English Channel in 1909. In October 1913, just short of his twenty-first birthday, The Aero Club of America awarded Sperry Federal Aeronautics Pilot License No. 11. This was after training at the aviation school of flight pioneer and aircraft designer Glenn Curtiss. He was the youngest licensed pilot in the United States.

Sperry's skills ran in the family. His father invented the nonmagnetic gyrocompass, which the US Navy quickly adopted because it overcame problems related to using a magnetic compass in very large steel vessels. The son realized that a lightweight gyroscopic stabilizer, using the same properties that enabled his father's gyrocompass, could keep an aircraft flying straight and level. He used a wind-driven generator, fitted on a wing, to generate electrical power to spin four gyroscopes—two to control lateral stability ("roll") and two to control longitudinal stability ("pitch")—and employed electrically powered servomotors to operate the aircraft's control surfaces. The pilot's only task was to maintain the aircraft's direction of flight with the rudder, with the Curtiss C-2 controlled by the steering wheels of the pilot and copilot. Additionally, the rudder could be locked to maintain the aircraft's straight trajectory. A key design challenge had been the size and weight of the gyroscopes and servomotors; Sperry compressed his kit into the size of a small suitcase that weighed only eighteen kilograms.[6]

In 1914, Sperry, with the French mechanic Emil Cachin, demonstrated the capabilities of his "autopilot" at the French

---

6   William Scheck, "Lawrence Sperry: Genius on Autopilot," HistoryNet, November 15, 2017, https://www.historynet.com/lawrence-sperry-autopilot-inventor-and-aviation-innovator/.

aircraft safety competition *La Concours de la Securité en Aéroplane*, which took place at Buc Aerodrome southwest of Paris, near Versailles. Some fifty-six aircraft took part. Not all impressed the judges or effectively demonstrated their new safety features. The *New York Times* published a report on the competition—"Long-Sought Aeroplane Stabiliser Invented at Last"—which described Sperry and Cachin's flight in their Curtiss flying boat:

> Standing up in his machine with both hands in the air, touching no levers, the young man told his mechanic to climb out on one of the plane's [wings]. The man did so, yet he had no more wish to die than you or I have. He calmly obeyed orders, stepped out on the wing as he might have sauntered out on the balcony of a house. Nothing happened. The machine maintained a horizontal course, while the ailerons did extra work. Lateral stability had been demonstrated. Next, the mechanic climbed aft toward the propeller some five or six feet. Again, the machine was undisturbed. Longitudinal stability had been demonstrated.[7]

---

7   Harold Hoeber, "Long-Sought Aeroplane Stabilizer Invented at Last," *The New York Times*, July 19, 1914, https://www.nytimes.com/1914/07/19/archives/longsought-aeroplane-stabilizer-invented-at-last-lawrence-b-sperry.html.

If you're wondering about the mechanic Cachin climbing "aft" toward the propeller, note that the Curtiss C-2 hydroplane had a single propeller mounted at the rear. The archived photographs illustrating the *New York Times* article depict an aircraft that closely resembles an open boat with wings attached. Apart from the gyroscopic gear in the well of the "boat" behind the seats of the pilot and copilot, there was very little to prevent Cachin from clambering about to his heart's content as you might in a small dinghy—assuming, which was clearly the case, that his nerves were up to the job.[8] There is a remarkable, grainy photograph elsewhere of Cachin standing nonchalantly on the wing on the biplane while Sperry holds his hands in the air to demonstrate that he is not controlling the plane's flight.[9]

The judges split the prize money of 40,000 francs (around £120,000 or $150,000 today) between many worthy competitors, with the Sperry Corporation receiving 5,000 francs.[10]

The gyroscopic stabilizer is still at the heart of many aircraft control systems. Using servomotors to operate control surfaces using input from various sensors was an innovation with obvious benefits, taking away much of the stress,

---

8 Hoeber, "Long-Sought Aeroplane Stabilizer."
9 MMAC, "Celebrating 100 Years of Autopilot," MONRONeYnews 5, no. 5, accessed April 23, 2024, https://www.esc.gov/MONRONeYnews/archive/Vol_5/TG/05_3.asp.
10 Scheck, "Lawrence Sperry: Genius."

concentration, and sheer physical effort of flying a plane, thus reducing the chances of pilot error. "Fly-by-wire" technologies, which take inputs from a pilot's physical manipulation of controls and turn them into electric or electronic signals that operate the aircraft's control surfaces via powered devices, have developed significantly from the 1950s onward. This took away the need for the complicated systems of cables, pulleys, and hydraulic pipes needed to translate the pilot's actions into different configurations of the plane's control surfaces. Such cables, pulleys, and hardware were bulky and weighty and needed additional backup systems in case of failure.

Replacing all this heavy, mechanical infrastructure with wiring brought obvious benefits in terms of weight—bringing cost savings in fuel and allowing fighter aircraft, in particular, to be made lighter and more agile. Now that the pilot's manual inputs converted into electrical (and, later, electronic) signals, they could also incorporate data from other sources. The fly-by-wire system would "understand" what the pilot intended by his or her actions—but could also factor in other information supplied by sensors to ensure that the pilot's actions did not push the aircraft beyond its capabilities. At a more mundane level, fly-by-wire also ensured a smoother flight than a human pilot, acting without such machine-aided augmentation, could deliver in canceling out the effect of turbulence. The iconic supersonic airliner Concorde was the first airliner to have an electrically controlled analog fly-by-wire control system. Its "full regime" autopilot and auto throttle allowed hands-off control. It also had an air data computer to monitor key aerodynamic measurements.

NASA's Dryden Flight Research Center developed the move to electronics and digital fly-by-wire (DFBW) in the 1970s and early '80s. They utilized a digital guidance and navigation computer and an inertial sensing unit that was initially developed for the Apollo moon landings. The system used multiple computers to control flight. NASA makes an interesting comment about this feature:

> ...Using the words "otherwise unstable" is fascinating: the use of computers does two key things for flight safety: it virtually eliminates the possibility of computer failure crippling an aircraft in flight, and it relies on the majority of the computers to instantly "vote" on the right control deflection to command. The computers can make the optimum control deflection choice quicker than a pilot and keep an otherwise unstable aircraft flying straight and true.[11]

---

[11] "Flight By Wire Control Systems," *Control Systems* (blog), May 29, 2018, http://www.oliver-control.com/FlightControlSystem/fly-by-wire-flight-control-system. More information about DFBW available at: NASA, "F-8 Digital...

The system was first tested in a modified F-8 Crusader carrier-based jet aircraft borrowed from the US Navy. Using the words "otherwise unstable" in the quote above from the NASA web archive is fascinating: the use of computers allowed human pilots to fly planes that were intrinsically unstable but far more maneuverable than a plane "stabilized" for human use. It also shows that NASA was allowing the "opinions" of several computers to dictate what action to take.

THREE KEY ISSUES

This brings three key issues about machine control and the separate issue of machine intelligence into focus. First, it is now commonplace to accept that machines and computing power can enable humans to do things they would be incapable of doing on their own. Second, it shows that there are existing situations where we have accepted that machines can make decisions with a speed and precision that humans cannot match; in many contexts, we have been forced to abandon the idea that human "instinct" will always be superior. Third, it introduces a concept of machine-driven knowledge that may not be perfect but can be "as good as it gets."

...Fly-By-Wire," Internet Archive, archived August 20, 2009, https://archive.org/details/299271main_EC77-6988_full.

With the F-8 Crusader controlled by DFBW, all the available data was fed through several computers, each focused on a slightly different aspect of the aircraft's performance, and the machines "voted"—in the blink of an eye—for a particular configuration of the aircraft's control surfaces and the thrust from its single Pratt and Witney J57 turbojet engine. A human pilot could not hope to match that decision-making process, and human "instinct" was counterproductive because the F-8 did not fly like a normal plane. The plane's control systems made use of the data and processing power available to it to make the split-second decisions that would keep the F-8 flying at supersonic speed and engaging an enemy fighter jet in aerial combat. In terms of real-time decision-making—even in what was for the human pilot a life-or-death situation—the machine-aided analysis was as good as it got.

THE PATH FORWARD

First, we develop new technologies; then we control and enhance those technologies by automating key processes related to safety and performance; then we see that the enhanced technology can deliver a superhuman level of performance. And though we are always nervous at first about surrendering control to machines, we learn that they are safer than the decision-making of more fallible human beings and enable things beyond normal human powers.

As our technologies become more and more complex—and more and more effective, leading to breakthroughs that were impossible and often unthinkable using older technologies—so our reliance on the machines that enable these new technologies increases. This is not a cause for alarm; it's just what the future will look like. Our technologies will enable other, more complex technologies that allow us to achieve increasingly dramatic advances. To be concerned about this is foolish. We might as well argue we should never have harnessed the power of steam, discovered how to generate electricity, or developed the silicon chip.

These technological developments will not only enable dramatic breakthroughs in science but also affect our social and political lives. With increasing volumes of data available for many aspects of our lives—our health; our homes and the many devices in them; our energy consumption; how, where, and when we travel; and how we make use of public facilities—it will be increasingly possible to use machines to analyze such data in real time and decide about the most efficient and effective use of public facilities and private resources. It is my belief we will soon use this data not only to make predictions and inform human decision-making but, increasingly, to allow machines to decide on our behalf.

CHAPTER 5

WHY INTELLIGENT SYSTEMS ARE THE BEST BET FOR OUR FUTURE

DEVELOPMENTS HAPPENING RIGHT NOW SHOW THE benefit of handing over management control over some areas of our society to machines. For example, there are now small rotary drones flying over fields of crops in the state of Gujarat, on the northwestern coast of India. The drones fly a few feet above the crops, following a pre-programmed path, using GPS navigation. Multispectral onboard cameras scan the crops below, capturing images across a wide range of wavelengths. These digital images provide a remarkable array of information—from soil analysis to plant height and density, levels of photosynthetic activity, weed cover, plant disease, and drought stress. The drones also record local environmental factors, such as wind, sun, and rain.

Buried in the soil beneath the crops, sensors record more information about soil PH, nutrients, and moisture levels. The Internet of Things (IoT) collects the data from the drones and the sensors in the soil, and machine intelligence analyze it to determine the actions that will produce the highest crop yield using the least resources: water, pesticides, fertilizers, labor. The resulting information is used to direct farming activity. Automated drip irrigation systems buried in the ground deliver precise amounts of water and nutrients to the roots of plants, minimizing loss through evaporation and precisely targeting the areas where they are most needed, considering a range of constantly changing parameters: climate conditions, the crops' stage of growth, plant density, soil properties, and the prevalence of pests and disease.

Unmanned vehicles that patrol the fields use machine imagery to distinguish between weeds and crops, destroying weeds with a variety of hyper-efficient techniques, including micro-spraying with selective herbicides, precision hoeing, and the use of electric pulses, pinpoint flames, and lasers. Farmers use drones to spray crops on a wider scale where it is needed, for example, in areas where disease or pests are taking hold. Spraying crops using drones is faster, more efficient, and safer than spraying by human beings. Drones can also be used for the initial sowing of some crops, planting "pods" containing seeds and the exact amount of fertilizer needed to ensure healthy growth. As the crops ripen, data from the drones instructs harvester robots to pick crops at the moment of perfect ripeness.

The data analyzed by machine intelligence informs and instructs humans and machines. Farmers access advice via automated chatbots, which advise them on the exact seed variety that will thrive on their soil and in their microclimate and the best fertilizers to use in the most efficient quantities. As the crop grows, the chatbots offer advice on a wide range of farming issues, analyzing data from previous calls using machine learning (ML) to better understand and predict farmers' needs and concerns. Smart apps give farmers estimates of the costs they will incur in bringing crops to harvest, predict crop yields, and forecast demand and market prices to help them optimize profits.

The growing volume of data generated by such "smart" farms, analyzed alongside medium- and long-term weather forecasts and the latest estimates of the impact of global warming, allows increasingly accurate predictions about future crop yields; future problems caused by pests, disease, and extreme weather; and the most productive crops to grow in different geographical areas.

The account outlined above is only futuristic. Gujarat has four agricultural universities and is a pioneer of high-tech agricultural practices. These smart farming techniques are already in use on various farms around the world. The state of Gujarat is mostly arid, with desert conditions in the northwest, though southern regions see heavy rains in the monsoon season. For most of the state's regions, minimizing the use of water is a key priority. Minimizing the use of fertilizers, pesticides, and herbicides is another, as is determining the most productive crop to grow in the different climatic conditions of the state's various regions.

On a national level, India's agricultural policy is very simple. A 2020 *The Times of India* article on the need for agricultural reform drew attention to the fact that agriculture contributed only 14 percent to the country's gross value added (GVA) but employed around 47 percent of the nation's workforce. Flipping that on its head, the country's nonagricultural sector contributed 86 percent of GVA with 53 percent of the workforce. The agriculture sector clearly needs to become more productive.[1] Low farm incomes reflect low levels of productivity. Small farmers running inefficient

---

1   Inderjeet Sambyal, "New Agricultural Policy: Let's Understand It in Totality," *Readers' Blog, The Times of India*, September 24, 2020, https://timesofindia.indiatimes.com/readersblog/third-eye/new-agricultural-policy-lets-understand-it-in-totality-26416/.

farms and earning little money dominate Indian agriculture. The country's food storage and distribution infrastructure also suffers from systemic inefficiencies.

There is also an opportunity here. India has the most arable land of any nation in the world, about 53 percent of which can grow crops, compared, for example, with the United States, where about 17 percent of total land mass is arable.[2] In 2018, the World Resources Institute forecasted we will need 56 percent more food than is currently produced to feed a forecast world population of ten billion by 2050.[3] India is already a significant exporter of food. A more productive agricultural sector would help guarantee food security not only for India, and drive an expanding export market which would raise farm incomes, improving the quality of life of almost half the nation's population. It would also help to future-proof the nation against the near certainty of increasing urbanization toward the megacities of the future, leading to the urgent need for a dwindling rural population to produce more food.

We can summarize the top imperatives for India's agricultural policy along these lines:

---

[2] "Arable Land by Country 2024," World Population Review, accessed April 23, 2024, https://worldpopulationreview.com/country-rankings/arable-land-by-country.

[3] Janet Ranganathan et al., "How to Sustainably Feed 10 Billion People by 2050, in 21 Charts," World Resources Institute, December 5, 2018, https://www.wri.org/insights/how-sustainably-feed-10-billion-people-2050-21-charts.

- Increase productivity per hectare.
- Make better use of inputs (water, fertilizer, pesticides).
- Improve efficiencies in the food supply chain.
- Raise the income of poor farmers.

The problem is that years of well intentioned but protectionist agricultural policies have led to what a 2020 Organisation for Economic Co-operation and Development (OECD) Monitor and Evaluation report on Indian agricultural policy described as a "price-depressing effect" on Indian farmers' produce. Although the government provides market price support to farmers and subsidizes their costs for water, electricity, fertilizers, and other inputs, the report concludes that these measures "do not offset the price-depressing effect of complex domestic regulations and trade policy measures." Put another way, the OECD calculates the overall effect of India's complex agricultural policies has been to reduce farmers' incomes below what they could be expected to earn for their product on the open market. In the meantime, the Indian government directly supports farmers through the direct benefit transfer system—support that might not be necessary if farmers could earn the full market price for their produce.

In terms of macro policy formulation, this looks like a simple problem: remove the policies that are leading to farmers receiving less than the international market value of their produce and create an environment that incentivizes investment in more efficient and productive farming techniques, including more education, training, and affordable access to high-tech farming solutions.

Under established policy, agricultural products could be sold only through government markets, or *mandis*, via commission agents. Goods were sold at auction in the *mandis*, with the government guaranteeing and subsidizing minimum prices. The commission agents acted as intermediaries between farmers and wholesalers and arranged transport and storage. The level of commission charged by agents was not always transparent and farmers had almost no bargaining power; the agents and wholesalers set prices, creating the risk of cartel pricing. Payments via the *mandi* system could also be slow. Commission agents might offer bridging loans to farmers, increasing the farmers' dependency on these middlemen.

In 2020, the Indian government of Prime Minister Narendra Modi introduced new agriculture reforms that he described as a "watershed moment," intended to raise farm incomes, reduce farmers' dependency on the *mandi* system and commercial agents, and increase their bargaining power. The policies were in harmony with the OECD report's recommendation that the government should "continue the initiatives to reduce domestic marketing inefficiencies...to thoroughly reform regulations and to foster more efficient and competitive markets."[4]

The new laws allowed farmers to sell directly to commercial buyers such as agribusinesses and supermarket chains and enabled private buyers to buy and stockpile produce—something that only government agencies were previously allowed to do. Experts expected that the introduction of private capital would drive new efficiencies in the country's notoriously inefficient food supply chain. The new policy would also make market information available to farmers via the internet, mobile apps, and electronic displays in *mandis*, helping farmers make informed decisions about the proper value of their goods, whereas previously they relied on information from a small network of family and friends and commission agents themselves. The minimum support price would remain in place.

The result of these welcome and forward-looking policy reforms? Farmers protesting against the new policies set up roadblocks around India and called for a nationwide strike. Despite the potential benefits of the new policies for farmers,

---

[4] Trade and Agriculture Directorate of the OECD, *Agricultural Policy Monitoring and Evaluation 2020* (Paris: OECD, 2020), 267–268, https://www.oecd-ilibrary.org/docserver/928181a8-en.pdf?expires=1720558325&id=id&accname=guest&checksum=9ACB0C5A38F4768276E66A8351C375BD.

many viewed them with suspicion, fearing they would strip away the relative securities of the old system and expose them to exploitation by large corporate forces.

"This is a death warrant for small and marginalized farmers," a protesting Punjabi farmer told the BBC as the first anniversary of the laws' introduction approached in September 2021. "This is aimed at destroying them by handing over agriculture and market to the big corporates."[5]

Farmers set up roadblocks and camped out on the outskirts of Delhi, within which the Indian capital of New Delhi is located. In January 2021, the protest turned violent, with farmers tearing down barriers, driving tractors through roadblocks, and storming the historic Red Fort in the heart of New Delhi. One farmer lost his life and many other protestors and police officers sustained injuries. Farmers kept up their protests as the year wore on. Reports indicated that dozens of farmers died due to exposure to extreme heat and cold while camping out in all seasons, and from COVID-19 during the pandemic. Public opinion shifted decisively in favor of the farmers when the son of a government minister drove his car into a crowd of protesters, killing eight people.[6]

---

5 "Bharat Bandh: India Farmers Strike to Press for Repeal of Laws," BBC, September 26, 2021, https://www.bbc.com/news/world-asia-india-54233080.
6 "Farm Laws: India PM Narendra Modi Repeals Controversial Reforms," BBC, November 18, 2021, https://www.bbc.com/news/world-asia-india-59342627.

In November 2021, with elections approaching in Punjab and Uttar Pradesh—both states that are heavily dependent on agriculture—the Indian government reversed its position and promised to repeal the new laws. Farmers were jubilant. Many experts were disappointed. "It's a blow to India's agriculture," one agricultural policy analyst told Reuters. "The laws would have helped attract a lot of investment in agriculture and food processing—two sectors that need a lot of money for modernisation."[7] That investment was now at risk. The Reuters report also quoted the head of a farmers' union saying that the new laws had offered farmers freedom from the forced reliance on middlemen—the commercial agents—and confirming that their repeal would leave them once again vulnerable to exploitation.[8]

I have used the example of India's agricultural policy because it is typical of the kinds of complex, sometimes highly inefficient pattern of subsidies, tariffs, import, and export restrictions, pricing policies, and other mechanisms that develop over time in many countries. As we saw earlier, such complex networks of policies can contain systemic inefficiencies that policymakers can be reluctant to

---

7 Mayank Bhardwaj and Rajendra Jadhav, "India's Modi Backs Down on Farm Reforms in Surprise Victory for Protesters," Reuters, November 19, 2021, https://www.reuters.com/world/india/indias-modi-repeal-controversial-farm-laws-2021-11-19/.

8 Bhardwaj and Jadhav, "India's Modi Backs Down."

remove—and any attempts that are made to reform the old, inefficient policies can be met with suspicion by the policymakers' constituents, often fueled by a lack of information and understanding. Even if the policymakers themselves have a complete grasp of the impact of their new policies, they may fail to explain these to their constituents. In his TV address announcing the Indian government's U-turn on agricultural policy, Prime Minister Modi acknowledged this, saying, "Despite several attempts to explain the benefits to the farmers, we have failed."[9]

The proposed new policies were certainly good policies, designed to modernize Indian agriculture, attract new investment to upgrade the country's wasteful food supply chain, and raise farm incomes. But they were perceived as threatening most of India's farmers, who were more comfortable with the existing inefficient and unrewarding but "secure" state-run system. Indian farmers had effectively been protected from the free market for years by the *mandi* system. Despite the system's glaring inefficiencies and potential for abuse, they feared exposure to the free market, even though the existing policies were preventing farmers from receiving the full rewards that the free market had to offer. In the end, the new policies fell victim to good

---

9   BBC, "Farm Laws: India PM."

old-fashioned politics—the risk of a protest vote against India's ruling party by disgruntled farmers. Nobody "won"—least of all the Indian economy.

THE INPUTTING OF ASSUMPTIONS

Let's go back to the example given at the beginning of the chapter regarding the growing impact of machine intelligence on farming practices. Intelligent systems are already being used to produce more high-quality crops, using fewer resources like water, fertilizers, pesticides, and so forth. Policy assumptions underlie that decision, but they are non-controversial—consensus exists on enhancing productivity while minimizing resource usage. But it is important to recognize that a policy decision has been made, one that affects how the algorithms work based on choosing to emphasize farming productively.

If, for example, there was no risk of run-off of fertilizers causing pollution of waterways, and if fertilizers were readily available and very cheap, we might choose to adjust our machines' algorithms so that the minimal use of fertilizer was no longer a priority. If we were not concerned about the effect of current pesticides and herbicides on biodiversity and human health, we might be happy to drench our crops with chemicals. We make several assumptions when we use machine intelligence to produce a desired outcome in even the most apparently straightforward instances. The adopted "policy" reflects the desired outcome of more productive and efficient crop production with minimal damage to the environment. Because there is general agreement about what is needed to raise crops productively and efficiently, using machine intelligence at this level is also noncontroversial. Farmers are happy to be guided by machines as to the crops they should plant and the amount of fertilizer and pesticide that they should use. They are happy for machines to devise the most efficient way of watering their crops, safeguarding a precious resource (experts estimate that around 70 percent of the world's fresh water is currently used in irrigation for agriculture).[10]

The nature of the decisions that machine intelligence is making on our behalf is understood. The machines are analyzing amounts of data that go far beyond human capabilities, deciding at incredible speeds, and considering detailed information—like the real-time levels of photosynthetic activity in the crops—that could only be estimated by humans after laborious research that led only to broad-brushstroke assumptions.

---

10 Anne Wilson, "Smart Irrigation Technology Covers 'More Crop per Drop,'" MIT News, October 25, 2023, https://news.mit.edu/2023/gear-lab-creates-affordable-user-driven-smart-irrigation-controller-1025.

There is an exact parallel here to the scientific method. The scientific community carries out research, makes hypotheses, and tests them against observable phenomena. Hypotheses that withstand experimental tests become candidates for being accepted as a potentially correct description of reality. Scientists review each other's work constantly, and what emerges becomes our current best description of how and why things are as they are. These are our current "truths."

There is also an acceptance that a radical discovery or a new way of seeing things may reveal those earlier truths to have been imperfect, just as our understanding of the universe has changed from the earth-centric theory of Ptolemy, which was refined by Al-Khwarizmi, through the solar-centric theory proposed by Copernicus and corroborated by Galileo, and on to Newton's laws and Einstein's theory of relativity.

Returning to the example of agriculture, we are happy (in fact, delighted) to allow machine intelligence to guide us in the practice of agriculture to produce food more efficiently and better follow certain key "strategic" policies (maximize crop production while minimizing various inputs, for example). We will become equally comfortable allowing machine intelligence to devise the policies we use to encourage the development of the most efficient and productive agricultural sector—modeling the various subsidies, price support mechanisms, taxes, and import and export restrictions we put in place to determine whether they are, in fact, delivering optimal results.

There are obvious potential barriers to this becoming a reality. In a later chapter, I will explore a number of them caused by the use of machine intelligence in various social contexts—welfare entitlement and benefit fraud, education, and others—and I will highlight the disasters that have occurred—as well as the successes. But I will argue that these early failures are teething problems we will resolve and move beyond and the successes are a true harbinger of the benefits machine intelligence offers in the policymaking space.

CHAPTER 6
WHAT EXACTLY DO WE MEAN BY ARTIFICIAL INTELLIGENCE ANYWAY?

"Intelligence is whatever machines haven't done yet."
—LARRY TESLER (COMPUTER SCIENTIST)

BEFORE GOING ANY FURTHER, I WANT TO ESTABlish a few frames of reference to what terms such as machine intelligence, artificial intelligence, machine learning, and the like mean. I don't intend to create any new, technical meanings for these terms, but simply to make sure that it is clear what I mean—and do not mean—when I use these terms in the coming pages.

To explore the potential of AI to contribute to the field of policymaking, we don't need to have a detailed understanding of how AI works or even precisely what is meant by the term, but we probably need to know what we *don't* mean by AI in this book.

The easy answer to what is meant by AI is that *it is not* what is known as "artificial general intelligence," which is a kind of human-like intelligence that can grasp new and complex situations, think conceptually, and weigh multiple factors before making a unique and "thoughtful" response. In the early days of AI research, it was assumed that to be intelligent, a machine must be intelligent in something like the human sense—a wide-ranging, general understanding. This conviction—that machines would develop general intelligence—gave rise, of course, to speculation about whether an intelligent machine would be conscious; for humans, intelligence, and consciousness are inextricably entwined, so it was understandably hard to imagine advanced intelligence would *not* be conscious and self-aware. This gave rise to alarmed debate about what this new machine consciousness would be like and whether it would be a threat to humanity.

The great Hungarian-American mathematician and computer scientist John von Neuman, writing in the 1940s, imagined a time when the creation by humans of what he called "automata" would develop in an "explosive" way: the clever automata would themselves create new machines that were more complex and advanced than themselves to better carry out certain functions, and things would quickly spiral out of control. Machines would develop in ways that humans could not even understand. Von Neuman called this a "technological singularity," by which he meant a state of affairs in which humanity would quickly become overwhelmed by the rate of change and unable to keep pace with the technological developments that were being made by non-human agents.

Science fiction author Vernor Vinge took the idea further, linking von Neumann's "technological singularity" to the concept of machines "waking up" and becoming conscious. At the Vision 21 Symposium held at the NASA Lewis Research Centre in 1993, Vinge argued it might become possible to develop computers "that are 'awake' and superhumanly intelligent," as he put it.[1] "To date, most controversy in the area of AI relates to whether we can create human equivalence in a machine. But if the answer is 'Yes, we can,' then there is little doubt that beings more intelligent can

---

[1] Vernor Vinge, "The Coming Technological Singularity: How to Survive in the Post-Human Era," (paper, Vision 21: Interdisciplinary Science and Engineering in the Era of Cyberspace, NASA Lewis Research Center, Cleveland, OH, December 1, 1993), 12, https://ntrs.nasa.gov/api/citations/19940022856/downloads/19940022856.pdf.

be constructed shortly thereafter."[2] With reference to von Neuman, Vinge continued:

> It's fair to call this event a singularity... It is a point where our old models must be discarded and a new reality rules. As we move closer and closer to this point, it will loom vaster and vaster over human affairs till the notion becomes a commonplace. Yet when it finally happens it may still be a great surprise and a greater unknown.[3]

Nick Bostrom, director of Oxford University's Future of Humanity Institute, in his 2014 book *Superintelligence*, gave this idea new impetus. Bostrom doesn't argue that we are on the brink of creating a superintelligence—which he defines as "any intellect that exceeds the cognitive performance of humans in virtually all domains of interest"—though he speculates that this may happen in this century.[4] Bostrom sees many potential routes to superintelligence, including dramatic advances in AI, "whole brain emulation" (creating a computational structure closely modeled on the human brain), the enhancement of human brainpower by selective

---

2   Vinge, "Coming Technological Singularity," 12.
3   Vinge, "Coming Technological Singularity," 12–13.
4   Nick Bostrom, *Superintelligence: Paths, Dangers, Strategies* (Oxford: Oxford University Press, 2014), 22.

breeding (which Bostrom agrees would be morally and politically challenging!), enhancing the human brain by machine interfaces, or some kind of burgeoning collective intelligence, including the concept of a web-based cognitive system (the idea that the internet, given enough additional engineering and computing power, might itself one day "wake up" and become self-aware and super intelligent).[5]

The existence of several potential routes to superintelligence gives Bostrom reason to believe that we will, in the future, create some kind of super-intelligent entity. What happens next is what interests him. Once an entity achieves superintelligence, it will have outstripped the intellectual capacity of the whole of humanity and there is no reason to suppose that it will not use this superintelligence to continue to develop its powers, without our help and in ways that we cannot even conceive of. Bostrom calls the moment at which a super-intelligent entity begins to further develop its "takeoff" and debates the timescale on which this might happen.

According to Bostrom, one conceivable scenario is that takeoff happens incredibly quickly:

> Fast takeoff scenarios offer scant opportunity for humans to deliberate. Nobody need even notice anything

---

[5] Bostrom, *Superintelligence*, 22–51.

unusual before the game is already lost. In a fast takeoff scenario, humanity's fate essentially depends on preparations previously put in place.[6]

The super intelligence will be beyond our control, from the moment it first comes into being, and if we have not made preparations in advance, we will only be able to hope that it wishes us no harm and can see some purpose in our continued existence.

This is scary stuff indeed. If you have seen the *Terminator* movies, you know all about "Skynet," the film's fictional, artificial neural network (more on such networks later in this chapter) that becomes conscious and turns malevolently on humanity, launching a nuclear attack when humans attempt to deactivate it.

It would be foolish to argue that we can never create a super-intelligent being, or to state we can comfortably control one when it comes to existence. But for this book, we can relax. We are a very long way from creating anything like a superintelligence, because we are still a very long way from creating any kind of AI that has anything like the capabilities of human intelligence. This is the probable minimum starting point for the creation of superintelligence, since an

---

6 Bostrom, *Superintelligence*, 64.

entity that is pretty smart, but not as smart as us, is unlikely to be able to create a superintelligence. We can take comfort from Michael Kanaan, the first US Air Force Chairperson for Artificial Intelligence, current Director of Operations for the USAF-MIT Artificial Intelligence Accelerator, and the author of the book *T-Minus AI*, in which he writes:

> It's important to understand that neither artificial general intelligence (AGI) nor superintelligence is within the reach or even the possible range of current AI design, or any currently known technology... For the foreseeable future, AI will not be able to create or solve anything from something that isn't there, from data it doesn't specifically have, or for something it hasn't specifically been designed and trained to do. AI has no intuitive or transferrable abilities—and, for now, it's not going to acquire those abilities.[7]

The AI technology we are concerned with in this book is not something unfathomable that may or may not be developed in a possible future. It is the here and now and, importantly, though it may not be smarter than us in terms

---

7   Michael Kanaan, *T-Minus AI: Humanity's Countdown to Artificial Intelligence and the New Pursuit of Global Power* (Dallas, TX: BenBella Books, 2020), loc. 111, Kindle.

of general intelligence, it can already do many things better than we can and also do many things that we currently cannot, even with the help of a great deal of computer power that is not aided by AI, including:

- Powering our in-car navigation systems.
- Recommending what song we may want to play next on our streaming software.
- Predicting what we are about to write on our computers and phones (and checking our spelling and grammar).
- Translating our spoken and written words into other languages.
- Driving our internet search engines.
- Showing us, to an unnerving extent, the advertisements that best reflect our interests and buying habits.
- Helping detect and treat our illnesses.
- Enabling chatbots that help us get the information and outcomes we want.

These now-commonplace uses of AI represent only a fraction of the technology's potential. AI is already inextricably woven into our daily life, and we are discovering hugely valuable new applications every day.

HOW WE GOT HERE

Let's take a brief look at the short history of AI to remind ourselves of the major breakthroughs and developments that have led to the current state of play. I used a famous quote at the head of this chapter from Larry Tesler: "Intelligence is whatever machines haven't done yet." Tesler was a pioneer in human-computer interfaces (and the inventor of "copy and paste"). He makes an important point very succinctly. Machine "intelligence" is making rapid progress and has very recently vaulted over several supposed hurdles in terms of things we imagined machines would never be capable of doing. However, because we imagined that human-like intelligence would be an unavoidable and essential attribute of such machines, we tend to disparage any AI capabilities that fall below this very high bar.

AI powers self-driving cars that can safely navigate busy urban environments and highways with ease and devises financial investment strategies that make hedge fund owners and their clients a great deal of money. But it is now recognized that these machines—or programs—are not really "intelligent." We are realizing that AI can make hugely valuable and unique contributions in many areas of intellectual endeavor without being as "intelligent" as we had originally imagined.

In 1956, an assistant professor of mathematics named John McCarthy proposed a summer research project into AI, approaching the Rockefeller Foundation for funding. He coined the term "artificial intelligence" in the lead-up to the project to clarify what the goal was and to "nail the flag to the mast," as he put it in an interview with the US media website CNET.[8] McCarthy's proposal to the foundation made the bold promise of "significant advance" in the project's course:

> We propose that a 2 month, 10 man study of artificial intelligence be carried out during the summer of 1956 at Dartmouth College in Hanover, New Hampshire. The study is to proceed on the basis of the conjecture that every aspect of learning or any other feature of intelligence can in principle be so precisely described that a machine can be made to simulate it. An attempt will be made to find how to make machines use language, form abstractions and concepts, solve kinds of problems now reserved for humans, and improve themselves. We think that a significant advance can be made in one or more of these problems if a carefully selected group of scientists work on it together for a summer.[9]

---

8 Jon Skillings, "Getting Machines to Think like Us (Q&A)," CNET, July 5, 2006, https://www.cnet.com/science/getting-machines-to-think-like-us/.
9 J. McCarthy et al., "A Proposal for the Dartmouth Summer Research Project...

McCarthy's co-proposers were Marvin Minksy (Harvard University), Nathaniel Rochester (IBM), and Claude Shannon (Bell Telephone Laboratories), all of whom became leading figures in computer science, AI, and information theory. But it would take more than "a summer" for significant advances to be made in AI.

Board games—and chess in particular—had always played a major role in early attempts to develop machine intelligence because they offer a self-contained problem to be solved and come with a predefined set of rules that must be followed (it probably helped that many mathematicians and computer scientists are avid chess players). John McCarthy's Dartmouth Project colleague, Claude Shannon, a gifted amateur chess player, in 1949 proposed that a computer could be programmed to play chess. In his paper, "Programming a Computer for Playing Chess," published in *Philosophical Magazine* in 1950, Shannon accurately hit one particular philosophical nail: "Chess is generally considered to require 'thinking' for skillful play," Shannon wrote. "[A] solution of this problem will force us either to admit the possibility of a mechanized thinking or to further restrict our concept of 'thinking.'"[10] What Shannon

---

...on Artificial Intelligence," Dartmouth, August 31, 1955, https://www-formal.stanford.edu/jmc/history/dartmouth/dartmouth.html.
10 Gary Kasparov, *Deep Thinking: Where Machine Intelligence Ends and Human Creativity Begins* (London: John Murray, 2017), 29.

was saying was that creating a machine that could play chess would force us to decide whether that machine was actually "thinking" or if several of what had always been thought of as "intellectual" challenges could be done without "thinking" in the human sense.

This reflected the position taken by the British cryptographer and pioneering computer scientist Alan Turing. In his seminal article "Computing Machinery and Intelligence" published in *Mind* in 1950, he posed the question, "Can machines think?" and proposed that the question was misguided. In Turing's words, this was a "meaningless" question. He proposed what he called the "imitation game" (which we now call the Turing test) and argued that if a machine could answer questions put to it by a human interrogator in such a way that the interrogator could not tell whether the answers were coming from a machine or human, then it should be conceded that the machine was showing intelligent behavior—and not worry about whether the machine was actually "thinking":

> May not machines carry out something which ought to be described as thinking but which is very different from what a man does?... I believe that in about fifty years' time it will be possible to programme computers...to make them play the imitation game so well that an average

interrogator will not have more than 70 per cent, chance of making the right identification after five minutes of questioning.[11]

Interestingly, Turing spent time at Bell Labs in 1943 during World War II, meeting Claude Shannon. Turing was working at the UK's Bletchley Park Government Code and Cypher School, looking for a way of decoding the encrypted communications of Nazi Germany and the Axis Powers. He visited Bell's headquarters in Greenwich Village, Manhattan, to study speech encryption, and discussed machine intelligence and the idea of creating a computer chess program that would involve some kind of "thinking" with Shannon. There is speculation that the two men's discussions informed Turing's thinking on machine intelligence and, no doubt, helped shape Shannon's ideas as well.[12]

Chess-playing computer programs were developed in the 1950s, but even non-elite human chess players could defeat them. With improvements in computing processing power and programming finesse, chess-playing programs advanced until the 1980s, by which time they offered a real challenge

---

[11] A. M. Turing, "Computing Machinery and Intelligence," *Mind* 59, no. 236 (October 1950): 435, 442, https://doi.org/10.1093/mind/LIX.236.433.

[12] Tula Giannini and Jonathan P. Bowen, "Life in Code and Digits: When Shannon Met Turing," *Proceedings of EVA London 2017* (July 2017): 51–58, https://doi.org/10.14236/ewic/EVA2017.9.

to human players. Commercial programs were often criticized for playing "ugly, inelegant chess," according to a 1984 review. However, these machines made fewer mistakes than humans and could compel the average person to play better chess.[13] In the late 1980s, the computing titan IBM, who had been exploring chess computing since the 1950s, decided it was time to get serious. They wanted to build a computer program that could defeat a world-chess champion.

A Taiwanese-American graduate student at Carnegie Mellon University, Feng-hsiung Hsu, had been working on a chess program called ChipTest, which won the World Computer Chess Championship in 1987. Feng-hsiung developed a new program called Deep Thought, in honor of the fictional computer of the same name in Douglas Adams's book *The Hitchhiker's Guide to the Galaxy*. Deep Thought defeated grandmaster Brent Larsen in a 1988 tournament match and won the World Computer Chess Championship, but it lost a 1989 two-game exhibition match against World Chess Champion Garry Kasparov, who won both games with ease. Feng-hsiung and his colleague Murray Campbell were then hired by IBM Research to work on Deep Blue, a nod to Feng-hsiung's Deep Thought program and IBM nickname Big Blue.

---

13 Emil Flock and Jonathan Silverman, "SPOC: The Chess Master," *Byte Magazine* 9, no. 3 (1984): 289.

Deep Blue was programmed with the rules of chess, the value ascribed to each piece, and a set of key parameters based on an analysis of thousands of grandmaster-level chess games. Additionally, they gave the computer a database of successful opening positions and endgames, along with an additional database of complete grandmaster games. For each move made by a human opponent, the program could search its database of all responses for the most effective response and, like a human grandmaster, could evaluate likely responses by its human opponent, looking several moves ahead—usually around six to eight moves, but potentially as many as thirty moves. Even a grandmaster of Kasparov's stature could "only" plan around twelve moves ahead.[14] Deep Blue could also avoid wasting processing power searching every game variation by using the alpha-beta search algorithm, which "prunes" search options by abandoning any search branch that suggests a move with a lower value than one already evaluated.

In 1996, IBM challenged Kasparov to a pair of six-game matches against Deep Blue.

Kasparov won the 1996 match four games to two. Deep Blue had proved itself a worthy opponent—but the human champion had won. Human intelligence was still in the ascendant, but humans were nervous. People had long

---

14 Kanaan, *T-Minus AI*, Ch. 7, loc. 1453ff.

regarded the ability to master complex board games like chess as the epitome of human intelligence. *Newsweek* magazine ran a cover story on a second match between Kasparov and Deep Blue in 1997 with the headline "The Brain's Last Stand." A victory by the machine was an existential threat to humanity's perception of itself as being at the pinnacle of creation, the most intelligent being in the known universe.

Deep Blue defeated Kasparov in the second match, becoming the first computer to defeat a world champion under tournament conditions. The IBM team had doubled the computer's power and speed since the 1996 match and added chess grandmasters to their team of computer scientists and engineers. They predicted victory for the machine. In the event, Kasparov won the first game and Deep Blue the second, with the next three games draws. In the final sixth game, Kasparov resigned to give Deep Blue a 3.5/2.5 victory.

Kasparov was distraught and accused IBM of cheating. This was not completely without foundation. In his book *Deep Thinking*, Kasparov recounts how he discovered many years later that the IBM team had programmed Deep Blue on the very morning of the final game to sacrifice a knight if Kasparov made an unusual move threatening the computer's piece, while Kasparov was certain the machine's logic would lead it to retreat. "Machines are not speculative attackers," wrote Kasparov. "They need to see a return on their investment...before they invest material." Kasparov had discussed the move earlier with his team and feared that someone—perhaps a Russian-speaking member of staff embedded in the staff of the Plaza Hotel, New York, where the Kasparov team was staying—had relayed the conversation to the IBM team. "[T]he odds of winning the lottery," Kasparov says in *Deep Thinking*, "are quite attractive in comparison to those of the Deep Blue team entering a specific variation I had never played before in my life into the computer's book on the very same day it appeared on the board in the final game."[15] One can see his point.

Kasparov became more philosophical as time went on. He could see he had not played at his best in the matches against Deep Blue and had perhaps been "psyched" because he was playing against a computer. He had looked for deep strategic intent at one point when the machine had, in fact, made a random move caused by a glitch in its software. In the last game, when Deep Blue sacrificed the knight, Kasparov became angry and despondent because he was convinced it would retreat. But he acknowledged that his match with Deep Blue marked the point at which computers were shown to outplay humans at chess, and the conclusion he ultimately draws is upbeat:

---

15 Kanaan, *T-Minus AI*, Ch. 10, loc. 3480ff.

Thousands of years of status quo human dominance, a few decades of weak competition, a few years of struggle for supremacy. Then, game over. For the rest of human history, as the timeline draws into infinity, machines will be better than humans at chess. The competition period is a tiny dot on the historical timeline. This is the unavoidable one-way street of technological progress in everything from the cotton gin to manufacturing robots to intelligent agents.[16]

EXPERTISE WITHOUT THOUGHT

The version of Deep Blue that defeated Kasparov in 1997 used a parallel array of thirty PowerPC 604e chips and 480 custom-designed "chess chips" designed by Feng-hsiung Hsu. Parallel computing enables the breakdown of processes into smaller parts that can be simultaneously analyzed, resulting in a massive speed-up of processing. The upgraded version of Deep Blue that defeated Kasparov in 1997 was capable of 200 million calculations per second—double the computer's speed available during its defeat by Kasparov the previous year.

That ability to search for an incredibly large number of moves in a relatively short period of time was to prove the

---

16 Kanaan, *T-Minus AI*, Conclusion, loc. 4100.

death knell of human chess superiority. It also proved that it was unnecessary for a machine to be "intelligent" in order to play chess—at least, not in the human, cognitive sense. All that was needed was an extensive database of moves and fast search capability. As Kasparov wrote:

> It took thirty years, but my beloved game was revealed to be too vulnerable to brute force fast searching to require strategic thinking from machines in order to defeat the best humans. As much work as went into tuning Deep Blue's evaluation function and training its openings, the depressing truth is that a few years and a new generation of faster chips later, none of it would have mattered very much. For better or worse, chess just wasn't deep enough to force the chess-machine community to find a solution beyond speed, something many among them lamented.[17]

The early—and now naïve—view that a chess-playing computer would need to be "intelligent" in something like the human sense had been thoroughly debunked, but at least humanity could console itself with the fact that Deep Blue was not a form of superintelligence. Deep Blue taught us the lesson that playing chess at the highest level, while

---

17 Kasparov, *Deep Thinking*, 73.

a remarkable mental achievement, could be replicated by a machine with a large database of winning chess moves and the capability to search that database quickly enough to play a winning game within a human timeframe. The AI used to develop Deep Blue is known as an "expert system" because it needs a human expert to program the machine with the rules of the game, a knowledge base (with Deep Blue, a huge database of successful chess moves by human chess players and some key parameters), and a set of "if-then" rules that instruct the machine what to do at every step.

CHAPTER 7

MACHINES THAT TEACH THEMSELVES

THE NEXT STAGE IN THE DEVELOPMENT OF AI WOULD take an alternative approach, removing computers' reliance on human input and allowing them to work things out for themselves from first principles. The results were astonishing, and this "machine learning" approach is now a dominant force in AI.

The concept of machine learning also goes back to the heady days of the 1950s. IBM's Arthur Samuel, a leading figure in computer gaming and self-learning programs, coined the term in 1959. The theory was that machine learning would allow a computer program to learn how to improve its performance of a particular task from its own experience.

The development of artificial neural networks (ANNs) is closely linked to machine learning. Individual nodes in ANNs behave like neurons in the human brain, which receive signals and send out a single electrochemical pulse in response. This simple activity underpins everything the human brain is capable of, exciting or inhibiting in other neurons connected in a neural circuit.

Artificial nodes (also known as neurons) behave similarly, receiving inputs as data that are then given mathematical weight based on their potential significance to what an algorithm is learning, and then passed on. Layers arrange neurons, with the earliest networks having three: an input layer, an intermediary or "hidden" layer, and an output layer. Each node multiplies the incoming data by the assigned weight and adds the products to produce a "total input." Nodes then produce an outgoing signal that might be directly proportional to the weighted input, the result of a mathematical function, or based on a pre-set threshold so that it only sends an output when the total input passes a certain value.

Networks can be "trained" to make sense of information by taking a known set of input data and replicating it as output by tweaking weightings and connections within the network to give an increasingly good match between the "training set" data fed into the network and the output. For example, a neural network designed for self-driving cars can recognize stop signs. Ideally, the network has a very large dataset of stop sign images in a wide variety of contexts and weather conditions, including damaged or partially concealed examples. The network's output is trained by adjusting the weights applied to each neuron so that the output becomes more and more accurate. Once trained—and this is the vital part—a network should then be able to identify an unseen image as being a stop sign or something else.

Another example is the analysis of people's medical data to predict the risk of heart disease. The training set would feature a very large number of people's medical data, labeled to reflect the individuals suffering from heart disease. Then, the network would train to recognize which sets of new data represented people who had, or had a high risk of, developing heart disease.

These examples are uncomplicated, but they represent extremely difficult challenges for machine learning. It is very hard, as you might imagine, to train a machine. For example, even if given a large dataset of images of cats, learning to differentiate—in every instance—between "cat" and "not cat" is a challenging problem. The machine does not know "catness" and must train to recognize which, and only which, complex combination of pixels fed into its input layer does indeed represent "cat." Given enough data, such networks have proven to be remarkably effective.

A very early type of learning algorithm for image recognition was developed in 1958 at the Cornell Aeronautical Laboratory by the psychologist Dr. Frank Rosenblatt, with funding from the US Navy. It recognized images from data fed to it via 400 photocells. It began life as a piece of software running on an IBM 704, but even that innovative computer was too slow to handle the volume of data available. Rosenblatt built his own custom-made machine called the Mark 1 perceptron, with banks of potentiometers physically adjusted by small electric motors to give each connection its appropriate weight (perceptrons are supervised learning algorithms modeled on biological neurons).

An article in the *New York Times* dated July 7, 1958 announced the launch of the perceptron, opening with some remarkable claims: "The Navy revealed the embryo of an electronic computer today that it expects will be able to walk, talk, see, write, reproduce itself and be conscious of its existence."[1] This is a perfect example of the then-current belief that a machine that could do human-like things would inevitably be able to do more human-like things—even become self-aware. Rosenblatt is quoted in the article

---

1   UPI, "New Navy Device Learns by Doing: Psychologist Shows Embryo of Computer Designed to Read and Grow Wiser," *The New York Times*, July 8, 1958, https://www.nytimes.com/1958/07/08/archives/new-navy-device-learns-by-doing-psychologist-shows-embryo-of.html.

saying that "the machine would be the first device to think as the human brain."

The article reported several predictions about the machine's capabilities, however, that would prove true in every detail:

> The Navy said the perceptron would be the first non-living mechanism "capable of receiving, recognizing and identifying its surroundings without any human training or control." [...] Later perceptrons will be able to recognize people and call out their names and instantly translate speech in one language to speech or writing in another language, it was predicted.[2]

It would take many years before ANNs could deliver on these bold predictions. Despite Rosenblatt's prescience and the demonstrable success of the Mark 1 perceptron, this new field of research would soon fall into relative neglect.

Rosenblatt's early perceptron consisted of three layers of neurons. Later neural networks experimented with additional intermediary layers that would receive the output of the previous layer, perform more operations, and pass on the newly weighted data to the next layer, before going on to the final output layer. Researchers referred to these as "deep" neural

---

2 UPI, "New Navy Device Learns."

networks. Two computer scientists from the Massachusetts Institute of Technology (MIT), Marvin Minsky (of Dartmouth Project fame) and Seymour Papert, wrote a book called *Perceptrons* that was published in 1969.[3] It offered a mathematical proof of a three-layered network's inability to compute some logical predicates, which meant it would be unable to discern certain types of patterns. The mathematical proof was, of course, rigorous, but applied to a perceptron with only one intermediary layer of nodes and where no node in that layer was connected to every one of the inputs. Connecting every input to a neuron or neurons was avoided in favor of simpler networks where "local" nodes were connected to limited numbers of inputs. But it was entirely possible, technically.

Minsky and Papert's book is seen as being responsible for the subsequent collapse in interest in this field of AI, known at the time as "connectionism" (because of its use of networks of connected neurons) in favor of a field of research called "symbolic AI" (also referred to as good old-fashioned AI, or GOFAI). The latter was based on the idea that it might be possible to represent human thought in a symbolic way and that machines could then manipulate those symbols in the same way humans could manipulate data, just as it had

---

3 Marvin L. Minsky and Seymour A. Papert, *Perceptrons: An Introduction to Computational Geometry* (Cambridge, MA: MIT Press, 1969).

proved possible to represent logic symbolically and then deal with those symbolic representations in a mathematical way to produce new insights and understandings.

Symbolic AI relies on humans giving computers instructions to solve a problem rather than allowing the computer to figure things out for itself. After the publication of *Perceptrons*, funding for machine learning dried up, leading to a decade-long "connectionist winter." This was one of several so-called AI winters when belief in its potential and funding for research into key areas of the field waned significantly. The debate as to whether Minsky and Papert deliberately set out to sabotage research into neural networks and machine learning in favor of symbolic AI is ongoing. It seems perverse for the authors to have defined a limited neural network—a single intermediary layer perceptron with local nodes—and then prove that it could not carry out certain functions. By the time the book was published—a decade after Rosenblatt's trailblazing work—multilayered neural networks had already been developed and were known to solve the functions that *Perceptrons* had shown a more basic network could not. Minsky and Papert argued that the enormous increase in complexity arising from multiple layers of interconnected nodes would mean that training such multilayered networks by tweaking the weights of the unimaginably complex web of connections between nodes across several layers would be hard. But this represents a challenge to be overcome, whereas their book seemed to imply that neural networks were inherently incapable of carrying out some key functions.[4]

However, some researchers kept the faith regarding neural networks, most notably the British-Canadian cognitive psychologist and computer scientist Geoffrey Hinton, a professor at Carnegie-Mellon University in Pittsburgh, Pennsylvania. In 1986 Hinton, together with psychologist David Rumelhart and computer scientist Ronald Williams (both at the University of California, San Diego), published a now-famous paper titled "Learning Representations by Back-Propagating Errors."[5]

In the early 1980s, Rumelhart had independently rediscovered an algorithm first invented in the 1970s by a postgraduate student at Harvard University, now known as the backpropagation algorithm. The training of a network depends on adjusting the various weights applied to data passing through nodes from the input until the output matches the input. In principle, one can manually adjust each weight and observe if the output moves closer to or further away from the desired result. This trial-and-error approach

---

4   Sebastian Schuchmann, "History of the First AI Winter," Medium, *Towards Data Science*, May 12, 2019, https://towardsdatascience.com/history-of-the-first-ai-winter-6f8c2186f80b.
5   David E. Rumelhart, Geoffrey E. Hinton, and Ronald J. Williams, "Learning Representations by Back-Propagating Errors," *Nature* 323, no. 6088 (1986): 533–536, https://doi.org/10.1038/323533a0.

becomes unfeasible because of complexity as Minsky and Papert had noted. Backpropagation had the potential to solve the problem by automating the process.

The backpropagation algorithm calculates the error between the actual output and the desired output and adjusts the weights between the layer beneath the output and the output layer itself to reduce that error. Then the algorithm computes the error between the previous layer of hidden nodes and adjusts those weights also—and so on, back through the layers of nodes in the opposite direction of the flow of data from input to output. This automated error change produced remarkable results. As Hinton wrote, modestly, in "How Neural Networks Learn from Experience" (published in 1992 in *Scientific American*), he and his colleagues had "popularized the algorithm by demonstrating that it could teach the hidden units to produce interesting representations of complex input patterns."[6]

The backpropagation algorithm gave neural networks powerful capabilities that Rosenblatt had glimpsed for his perceptron: the ability to learn from experience without being given a set of instructions by humans, even when that "experience" came as an intricate set of data. This opened up

---

6   Geoffrey E. Hinton, "How Neural Networks Learn from Experience," *Scientific American* 267, no. 3 (September 1992): 146–147, https://doi.org/10.1038/scientificamerican0992-144.

the possibility that machines could learn to do things that humans could not figure out via programming.

The perfect example of an AI problem that had eluded symbolic AI was language translation—one of the holy grails of AI research. Researchers had attempted to program computers with syntax and grammar rules to enable the machine to translate sentences from one language to another using the symbolic AI approach. The huge difficulties involved in devising a set of rules and instructions that could cope with the vagaries of how real people actually use language defeated these attempts. Famous, possibly apocryphal stories imply that early computer programs translated the English sentence "The spirit is willing, but the flesh is weak," into the Russian sentence "The vodka is good, but the meat is rotten." Another example was "Out of sight, out of mind" getting translated as "invisible, insane." Meaning is everything…and we can't write a program for meaning. Which brings us back to the problem of machines doing "intelligent" things, like translating from one language to another, without actually being intelligent—a problem machine learning was about to solve.

PROCESSING BIG DATA

It's important to stress that machine learning is not the exclusive province of ANNs. They are proving to be incredibly good at machine learning, but "statistical learning" was an antecedent to machine learning using ANNs, and it is still very much in use today.

For example, in the late 1980s, the IBM Thomas J. Watson Research Center began experimenting with a machine translation system that essentially taught itself to translate from one language to another via the input of a very large number of examples of texts that had already been translated by humans. Once it had been trained and given a new piece of text (or "string") in one language, the machine would search its database of all target strings for the original in the target language with the highest probability of being a correct translation.

The system was based on statistical techniques first proposed in the 1940s, a time when there were not enough computer resources available for the technique to be tested. In 1988, IBM started a project known as Candide hoping that the increases in computing power over the intervening years had made the idea worth revisiting. For their initial database, they used the proceedings of the Canadian Parliament, which are recorded in both English and French. The research team fed over two million pairs of sentences from these records into their computer. The results were hopeful, though far from perfect, and suggested that using the statistical method on enormous volumes of accurate, paired translations could have great potential.

In 2007, Google switched from SYSTRAN, one of the oldest rule-based machine translation technologies, to its own statistical learning system. The year prior to the full rollout of the new system, a Google research scientist posted an announcement on the *Google Research* blog regarding the launch of a statistical learning-based Arabic–English and English–Arabic machine translator:

> Because we want to provide everyone with access to all the world's information, including information written in every language, one of the exciting projects at Google Research is machine translation. Most state-of-the-art commercial machine translation systems in use today have been developed using a rules-based approach and require a lot of work by linguists to define vocabularies and grammars.
>
> Several research systems, including ours, take a different approach: we feed the computer with billions of words of text, both monolingual text in the target language, and aligned text consisting of examples of human translations between the languages. We then apply statistical learning techniques to build a translation model.[7]

---

7   Franz Och, "Statistical Machine Translation Live," *Google Research* (blog), Google, April 28, 2006, https://research.google/blog/statistical-machine-translation-live/.

In 2016, Google introduced a neural network-based translation system to supersede the previous statistical learning system. The same year, the product lead for Google Translate put out this statement:

> In 10 years, Google Translate has gone from supporting just a few languages to 103, connecting strangers, reaching across language barriers and even helping people find love. At the start, we pioneered large-scale statistical machine translation, which uses statistical models to translate text. Today, we're introducing the next step in making Google Translate even better: Neural Machine Translation.
>
> Neural Machine Translation has been generating exciting research results for a few years and in September, our researchers announced Google's version of this technique. At a high level, the Neural system translates whole sentences at a time, rather than just piece by piece. It uses this broader context to help it figure out the most relevant translation, which it then rearranges and adjusts to be more like a human speaking with proper grammar. Since it's easier to understand each sentence, translated paragraphs and articles are a lot smoother and easier to read. And this is all possible because of end-to-end learning system built on Neural Machine Translation,

which basically means that the system learns over time to create better, more natural translations.[8]

One of the key drivers of the success of machine learning using ANNs has been the availability of huge amounts of data in digital form, driven primarily by the growth of the internet and the use of smartphones. In his 1992 article in *Scientific American*, Geoffrey Hinton said that ANNs trained using the back-propagation algorithm had proved to be "surprisingly good at training networks with multiple layers to perform a wide variety of tasks. It is most useful in situations in which the relationship between input and output is non-linear and training data are abundant."[9]

This new availability of "big data" was a key part of the growing success of machine learning by ANNs. A 2002 study by the University of California, Berkeley, estimated that the total amount of data produced in print, film, magnetic, and optical storage media worldwide was around five exabytes (five billion gigabytes).[10] According to the International Data Center (IDC),

---

8   Barak Turovsky, "Found in Translation: More Accurate, Fluent Sentences in Google Translate," *The Keyword* (blog), Google, November 15, 2016, https://blog.google/products/translate/found-translation-more-accurate-fluent-sentences-google-translate/.
9   Hinton, "How Neural Networks Learn," 147.
10 Nikki Swartz, "The Myth of the Paperless Office," *Information Management Journal* 38, no. 1 (January/February 2004): 10, https://go.gale.com/ps/i.do?id=GALE%7CA112859556&sid=googleScholar&v=2.1&it=r&linkaccess=...

the amount of data created and replicated worldwide in 2020 was over sixty-four zettabytes (6.4 trillion gigabytes)—a thousand-fold growth in less than twenty years. IDC forecasted a further 23 percent growth by 2025, much of this driven by the Internet of Things, security cameras, and social media.[11]

How much data can and should be stored is becoming a pressing issue, but from the perspective of data availability for machine learning training sets, we have opened the floodgates, and more data leads to better performance. As Josh Estelle, a software engineer for Google Translate, told *The Atlantic* in 2013, this new availability of huge amounts of data meant that even quite basic algorithms thought to have become outdated could now deliver very good results:

You can take one of those simple machine-learning algorithms that you learned about in the first few weeks of an AI class, an algorithm that academia has given up on, that's not seen as useful—but when you go from 10,000 training examples to 10 billion training examples, it all starts to work. Data trumps everything.[12]

...abs&issn=15352897&p=AONE&sw=w&userGroupName=oregon_oweb&aty=ip.

11 TechDay, "The World Generated 64.2 Zettabytes of Data Last Year—But Where Did It All Go?," DataCenterNews, March 26, 2021, https://datacenternews.asia/story/the-world-generated-64-2-zettabytes-of-data-last-year-but-where-did-it-all-go.

12 James Somers, "The Man Who Would Teach Machines to Think," *The Atlantic*, November 2013, https://www.theatlantic.com/magazine/archive/2013/11/the-man-who-would-teach-machines-to-think/309529/.

CHASING THE HOLY GRAIL OF REINFORCEMENT LEARNING

In 2016, a BBC *Newsnight* documentary covered a development it described as potentially "the biggest step forward in artificial intelligence and technology for decades."[13] The documentary featured AlphaGo, a revolutionary piece of software developed by the London-based company DeepMind Technologies.

Demis Hassabis founded DeepMind in 2010 by (with partners Shane Legg and Mustafa Suleyman) before being bought by Google in 2014. Hassabis grew up in North London, the son of a Greek Cypriot father and a Chinese Singaporean mother. He began playing chess at the age of four and became an International Chess Federation master at thirteen. He would later win the Mind Sports Olympiad "Pentamind" event five times between 1998 and 2003. When Hassabis was still a schoolboy, he bought his first computer—a ZX Spectrum manufactured by the UK's pioneering Sinclair Research company—with winnings from chess competitions and then taught himself to program. "Ever since then," Hassabis said in the documentary *AlphaGo*, "I felt that

---

13 BBC, "AlphaGo and the Future of Artificial Intelligence," *BBC Newsnight*, originally aired March 3, 2016, YouTube video, 0:07:44 (quoted material 0:00:48–0:00:57), https://www.youtube.com/watch?v=53YLZBSS0cc.

computers were this sort of magical device that could extend the power of your mind."[14]

At sixteen, Hassabis had completed both the UK's A-level and the more advanced S-level examinations and was accepted by the University of Cambridge to study computer science. The university asked him to take a gap year because of his age; Hassabis worked for a video game company. After being awarded a *double first* (the highest honors degree achievable) at Cambridge, he went back into video game production, working as the lead AI programmer on *Black and White*. The games industry was at the forefront of AI research, using the technology to allow computer-driven "non-player characters" to interact with players in real time—and learning from experience to change behaviors as the game progresses.

After spending a decade in video games, Hassabis returned to academia to study for a doctorate in cognitive neuroscience at University College London (UCL). "I switched out of that [video games] back to academia and neuroscience," Hassabis told *The Verge* magazine in 2016, "because I felt around the mid-2000s that we'd gone as far as we could

---

14 *AlphaGo*, directed by Greg Kohs, featuring Lee Sedol (New York, NY: Moxie Pictures, 2017), 00:01:39–00:01:49, https://www.alphagomovie.com/. Quotes in this chapter regarding AlphaGo are from the film unless otherwise referenced.

trying to sneak in AI research through the back door while you're actually supposed to be making a game."[15]

After his PhD, Hassabis worked as a researcher in neuroscience and artificial intelligence at MIT and Harvard University, and then back at UCL before reentering the commercial world by founding DeepMind in 2010. From the outset, the founders set themselves the challenge of developing an AI program that could challenge the world's best players at the ancient Chinese game of Go, dubbing the new program AlphaGo:

> Go has always been the pinnacle of perfect information games. It's way more complicated than chess in terms of possibility, so it's always been a bit of a holy grail or grand challenge for AI research, especially since Deep Blue. And you know, we hadn't got that far with it, even though there'd been a lot of efforts.[16]

Deep Blue had beaten Kasparov at chess, but the ancient game of Go presented an altogether different level of challenge. In contrast, chess is played on a board of eight-by-eight

---

15   Sam Byford, "DeepMind Founder Demis Hassabis on How AI Will Shape the Future," *The Verge*, March 10, 2016, https://www.theverge.com/2016/3/10/11192774/demis-hassabis-interview-alphago-google-deepmind-ai.
16   Byford, "DeepMind Founder."

squares, while Go is played on a board of nineteen-by-nineteen squares. Players put stones on any of the 361 intersections on the board's lines. Whereas there are an average of thirty or more possible moves for a chess player at each turn, there are two hundred to three hundred possible moves in Go. Researchers have calculated that by the end of a typical game, chess will have a total of 10^{120} game variations compared to 2×10^{170} variations in Go.[17] As Hassabis told *BBC Newsnight* in a 2016 documentary, "The game of Go has just two rules, but out of those rules comes a profound complexity. There are more possible board configurations in the game of Go than there are atoms in the universe."[18]

Go's unimaginable number of moves require players to develop what had always been considered an exclusively human intuition about the game by taking in the overall disposition of the pieces on the board at a glance and to "sense" the most advantageous move, as Hassabis explained:

> If you took all the computers in the world and ran them for a million years, that wouldn't be enough computer power to calculate all the possible variations. If you ask

---

17 Michael Kanaan, *T-Minus AI: Humanity's Countdown to Artificial Intelligence and the New Pursuit of Global Power* (Dallas, TX: BenBella Books, 2020), loc. 1566, Kindle.
18 BBC, "AlphaGo and the Future," 00:01:18–00:01:28.

a great Go player why they played a particular move, sometimes, they will just tell you it felt right. So, we have to come up with some kind of clever algorithm to mimic what people do with their intuition.[19]

The way DeepMind went about this challenge was revolutionary. The team took the basic principle of reinforcement learning in which an "agent" learns by trial and error based on a system of rewards or punishments. Previous attempts to train neural networks using reinforcement learning had run into problems of "unstable learning," including episodes of "catastrophic forgetting" that were as problematic as they sound. DeepMind developed the Deep Q-Networks (DQN) algorithm to estimate the total reward the agent can expect from any action. By storing all the agent's experiences and randomly sampling and replaying them, the algorithm overcame previous issues of learning instability. This combination of reinforcement learning and deep learning to use neural networks was dubbed "deep reinforcement learning."[20]

The team tested their new algorithm on early arcade games such as *Space Invaders* and *Breakout*. In a talk at

---

19 *AlphaGo*, Kohs, 00:08:40–00:08:54.
20 David Silver, "Deep Reinforcement Learning," *DeepMind* (blog), Google, June 17, 2016, https://deepmind.google/discover/blog/deep-reinforcement-learning/.

Oxford University's Radcliffe Camera featured in the *AlphaGo* film, Hassabis described what happened as the algorithm learned to play the game:

> Virtual environments and games. We think they're the perfect platform for developing and testing AI algorithms. Games are very convenient in that a lot of them have scores, so it's very easy to measure incremental progress. So I'm going to show you a few videos of the agent system, the AI. So let's start off with Breakout. So here you control the bat and ball and you're trying to break through this rainbow-colored wall. The agent system has to learn everything for itself, just from the raw pixels. It doesn't know what it's controlling; it doesn't even know what the object of the game is. Now, at the beginning, after one hundred games, you can see the agent is not very good. It's missing the ball most of the time. But it's starting to get the hang of the idea that the bat should go towards the ball. Now, after three hundred games, it's about as good as any human can play this and pretty much gets the ball back every time. We thought, "Well, that's pretty cool." But we left the system running for another two hundred games, and it did this amazing thing. It found the optimal strategy was to dig a tunnel around the side and put the ball round the back of the wall. The researchers working

on this—the amazing AI developers—well, they're not so good at Breakout, and they didn't know about that strategy. So, they learned something from their own system, which is, you know, pretty funny and quite instructive, I think, about the potential for general AI.[21]

Hassabis's use of the term "general AI" reflects the move away from what is called "narrow AI"—which was developed to solve one particular problem—and toward programs that can apply learning and insight to a wide range of unique problems. "The whole beauty of these types of algorithms," says Hassabis, "is because they are learning for themselves, they can go beyond what we as the programmers know how to do and allow us to make breakthroughs in areas of science and medicine."

The early iteration of AlphaGo taught itself games like *Breakout*, *Space Invader*, *Seaquest*, *Beamrider*, *Enduro*, and *Q*bert* and outperformed humans.[22] The programmers' approach to the far more complex game of Go was based around two deep neural networks: a "policy" network that was initially trained using "supervised learning"—that is to

---

21 *AlphaGo*, Kohs, 00:01:49–00:02:59.
22 Kyle Wiggers, "A Look Back at Some of AI's Biggest Video Game Wins in 2018," *VentureBeat*, December 29, 2018, https://venturebeat.com/ai/a-look-back-at-some-of-ais-biggest-video-game-wins-in-2018/.

say, by being given a training set of human games to learn from. The policy network's job was to narrow the search by selecting moves with the best probability of success. The second network, the "value" network, was trained to predict the winners of games that the policy network played against by calculating the probability of winning from any position. The outputs of these two networks were combined with a Monte Carlo tree search. This is an algorithm that uses random sampling to predict outcomes for the very large number of options in the "game tree"—a hugely complex description, visualized as the branches and twigs of a tree, of all the ways a game could play out.[23]

Initially trained using one hundred thousand games between strong amateurs that the DeepMind team downloaded from the internet, the policy network was taught to mimic the play of gifted human players. The network then improved through reinforcement learning, playing some thirty million games against itself. By the end of this process, it could beat earlier versions of itself 80 to 90 percent of the time.[24]

Hassabis emailed the European Go champion, the Chinese-born French national Fan Hui, and asked if he could

---

23 David Silver et al., "Mastering the Game of Go without Human Knowledge," *Nature* 550, no. 7676 (2017): 354–359, https://doi.org/10.1038/nature24270.
24 BBC, "AlphaGo and the Future," 00:02:47–00:03:43.

help in the development of AlphaGo. Fan recounts how he imagined the DeepMind team might want to implant electrodes in his skull and scan his brain while he was playing and was relieved to find that what the team actually had in mind was his taking on the machine in a five-game set. "Oh, it's okay. Just a program!" Fan says in his heavily accented but fluent English in *AlphaGo*. "So, it will be easy to play!" At the time there were several Go programs on the market, but they were no competition for the best human players. Fan was supremely confident.

In October 2015, Fan played five matches against AlphaGo. The program won five games to nil. A computer program had never before defeated a professional player.

"I feel something very strange," said Fan. "I lose with a program, and I don't understand myself anymore." Fan had been playing Go since he was a child. Top players say that every Go player reveals something quite profound about themselves in their style of play; losing to a computer affected Fan's concept of who he was as a person. But on reflection, he became more philosophical. After walking the streets of London for an hour after the match, he returned to DeepMind's headquarters in London's King's Cross: "I'm not happy to lose the game. But I will be happy [to have played a part in] history."

The Go community ranked Fan as a 2nd dan player. The very best players are ranked 9th dan. The Go community was quick to believe that AlphaGo would not have won against a top-ranked player. The DeepMind team invited Fan to join as a consultant and he played Go against AlphaGo incessantly, probing for weaknesses. Eventually, he found one. There were some areas of play that the machine seemed to lack experience in. The team talked about "lumps" of knowledge the program was missing. If it entered one of these areas, the team referred to it as becoming "delusional."

After the victory against Fan Hui, the DeepMind team challenged South Korean Lee Sedol, the world Go champion and winner of eighteen world championships, to a five-game match in October 2016. The team was doubtful they had the time to fix AlphaGo's rare lapses into "delusion." The contest between AlphaGo and Lee took place at the Four Seasons Hotel in Seoul, South Korea. Lee, naturally, was confident of winning. The game, like Kasparov's matches against Deep Blue, had caught the attention of the world's media. Go enthusiasts obsessively followed the game, and even non-players found it intriguing.

DeepMind team member Aja Huang placed stones on the board following AlphaGo's instructions. Lee's wife and young daughter were in the audience watching the game. As the first match developed, AlphaGo played aggressively, like a top professional player, its moves often surprising expert commentators.

Lee's playing style was impassive, his expression slightly mournful. After one surprising move by AlphaGo, Lee glanced at the face of his "opponent," trying to read his intentions. But Aja was not Lee's opponent; he was just moving the stones as directed by AlphaGo. AlphaGo itself was unreadable. About halfway into the match, AlphaGo made a particularly challenging move. Lee's jaw dropped open. He blinked several times and put his fingers briefly to his temple; then he cupped his chin in his hand and stared intently at the board. The DeepMind team noted that AlphaGo at that point in the game was searching fifty to sixty moves ahead. A little later in the game, AlphaGo made a move that was initially deemed a mistake—but the experts, who were doing quite complex calculations to see which player was gaining more "territory" by surrounding it with their pieces, could see that AlphaGo was ahead and in a winning position. Soon thereafter, Lee resigned.

At the subsequent press conference, laughing a little nervously, Lee admitted he was surprised and felt he had made mistakes early on that had stayed with him throughout the game. He hadn't expected that "AlphaGo would play the game in such a perfect manner." However, he was a seasoned professional and felt sure he would not be thrown by his loss and put the odds of his winning the match at 50/50, adding graciously, "I would like to express my respect to the programmers for making such an amazing program."

In the second game, Lee played more cautiously. At one point, he took a cigarette break—something he did in games when he wanted to collect his thoughts. On his return, he found that AlphaGo had made a move (move thirty-seven) that the commentators described as "totally unthinkable."

Fan Hui, who was watching the game as an observer, said that the move was "a big shock." When Lee got back to the table and saw the move, he frowned, then smiled a little as if he thought AlphaGo had made an error. Then he sat back in his chair, tugging pensively at his lower lip, thinking about his next move for a full twelve minutes (when he normally took only one or two):

What?! Normally, humans, we never play this one—because it's bad! It's just bad. We don't know why; it's bad! [but soon realized] The more I see this move, I feel something changed. Maybe for humans we think it's bad. For AlphaGo, why not? This move is very spatial. Because with this stone, all the stones played before [...] work together. [They] connect. It looks like network; link everywhere. It's very special; very special.

He fought on, but eventually resigned again. After the game, he said "I thought AlphaGo was based on probability calculation and that it was merely a machine. But when I saw this move, I changed my mind. Surely AlphaGo is creative! This move was really creative and beautiful."

In the third game, Lee changed his style and attacked more aggressively. It was not his natural style and AlphaGo cruised to victory as Lee looked more and more agitated. At the press conference after this game, Lee apologized for not playing "better or smarter" and feared he had "disappointed too many of you" by seeming powerless in the face of AlphaGo's onslaught: "I never felt this much pressure; this much weight."

AlphaGo emerged as the victor with a 3–2 score, winning the match. In game four, Lee was more relaxed, with nothing to lose and pride to be regained. He achieved the impossible and found a move that confounded AlphaGo.

With the game evenly poised, Lee found a move described by another Go professional as "the hand of God" that drove a wedge between AlphGo's positions on the board. AlphaGo seemed to go into meltdown. The team noted that the software showed that it had estimated that there was only a one in ten thousand chance of any human playing Lee's move. Experts believe that when such a brilliant move is made—a completely unexpected move that opens up perhaps only one precise and certain path to victory and where all other paths will fail—the Monte Carlo search system, which is based on sampling, might be "missing the needle in the haystack that leads to a near certain loss" as one fifth dan amateur Go player wrote at the time.[25]

In the absence of any clear path to victory, AlphaGo made a series of apparently random moves and eventually resigned, as it was programmed to do when it estimated its chances of winning at less than 20 percent. Lee had not found a magic bullet that would always defeat AlphaGo. The fifth game was close, but AlphaGo played brilliantly again, moving inexorably toward Lee's resignation after a closely contested opening.

Many of AlphaGo's moves looked strange to the human eye. "This is what 10 or 11 dan play looks like," said Frank Lantz, Director of New York University's Game Center. "It looks weird, and we don't quite understand it."

One theory was that, since Go was a game of territory, humans had become overly obsessed with holding and expanding the obvious areas of the board under their control—but a player who has more territory scattered around the board in tiny pockets would still be the winner. AlphaGo, with its focus on winning—even by the smallest margin—was perhaps less concerned with obvious territory and

---

[25] David Ormerod, "Lee Sedol Defeats AlphaGo in Masterful Comeback—Game 4," Go Game Guru, accessed April 23, 2024, https://web.archive.org/web/20161116082508/https:/gogameguru.com/lee-sedol-defeats-alphago-masterful-comeback-game-4/.

more focused on the technicalities of winning. Go players felt that AlphaGo had made a real and lasting contribution to the game.

"What surprised me the most was that AG showed us that moves humans may have thought are creative, were actually conventional," said Lee. A post-doctoral researcher at Boston College, Changhoon Oh, carried out interviews in Seoul to gauge people's reactions to the Korean champions' loss. Some felt that AlphaGo was unpleasantly ruthless and emotionless—inhuman. Others thought that the program had opened up new possibilities: "People learn their strategies from their teachers. But AlphaGo discovered new ways a human teacher cannot suggest. I think we should learn from AlphaGo's moves."[26]

Lee's victory in the fourth game has become legendary, and he reflects in *AlphaGo*:

> It seemed like we humans are so weak and fragile, and this victory meant we could still hold our own. As time goes on, it will probably be very difficult to beat AI. But winning this one time, it felt like it was enough. One time was enough.

---

26 Changhoon Oh, "Us vs. Them: Understanding Artificial Intelligence Technophobia over the Google DeepMind Challenge Match," accessed April 23, 2024, http://www.changhoonoh.com/?p=12523.

After their victory against Lee, the DeepMind team moved on to further advances. They developed a new program, AlphaGo Zero, that taught itself to play from scratch without the input of a set of human games. Writing in the October 2017 issue of *Nature*, DeepMind authors headed by David Silver (and including Fan Hui and Demis Hassabis) described the new program:

> First and foremost, it is trained solely by self-play reinforcement learning, starting from random play, without any supervision or use of human data. Second, it uses only the black and white stones from the board as input features. Third, it uses a single neural network, rather than separate policy and value networks. Finally, it uses a simpler tree search that relies upon this single neural network to evaluate positions and sample moves, without performing any Monte Carlo rollouts. To achieve these results, we introduce a new reinforcement learning algorithm that incorporates lookahead search inside the training loop, resulting in rapid improvement and precise and stable learning.[27]

It had taken several months to train AlphaGo Lee, the version of the program that had defeated Lee Sedol. After only

---

27 Silver et al., "Mastering the Game," 354.

thirty-six hours of training, AlphaGo Zero was outperforming AlphaGo Lee. The new program was not only meaner, it was leaner, running on only four processing units, whereas AlphaGo Lee had required forty-eight distributed across several machines.

As an experiment, the team trained a neural network with the same architecture as AlphaGo Zero, using supervised learning based on a dataset of human games of Go. This produced better initial performance and was better at predicting human moves, but the self-taught version outperformed it overall, defeating it within twenty-four hours of self-learning. The self-taught AlphaGo Zero was devising its own superior strategy of play. The team's article in *Nature* concluded:

> Humankind has accumulated Go knowledge from millions of games played over thousands of years, collectively distilled into patterns, proverbs and books. In the space of a few days, starting tabula rasa, AlphaGo Zero was able to rediscover much of this Go knowledge, as well as novel strategies that provide new insights into the oldest of games.[28]

---

28 Silver et al., "Mastering the Game," 358.

People will harness this computing power for more than just playing games. In *AlphaGo*, Astronomer Royal of Cambridge University Martin Rees forecasts humans will become increasingly comfortable allowing AI to analyze data and draw its own conclusions:

> Machines will have the capability not only to crunch through a huge amount of data, but also to analyze it intelligently. Just as in the Go games, the machine made moves that surprised even the experts. And, eventually, the machines will gain our confidence because we will see that very, very often they make a better guess than we could have made as humans.[29]

Artificial neural networks may or do not represent the future of AI. Researchers neglected the technology in the 1970s before experiencing a great resurgence of interest. It is always possible that some other field of AI will emerge or re-emerge that will take AI to new heights. Machine learning itself—though likely to play an increasingly important role in the development of AI—is not the be-all and end-all. Many invaluable uses of AI are based on supervised learning, or statistical techniques, or Good Old-Fashioned symbolic AI.

---

29 *AlphaGo*, Kohs, 01:20:26–01:20:45.

What is certain is that AI—in some form or other—will play an increasingly vital role in enhancing human decision-making and, sometimes, replacing human decision-making.

CHAPTER 8
WHEN AI GOES WRONG

A S THE TECHNOLOGY ADVANCES, MACHINES WILL control not only other machines—elevators, cars, airplanes, nuclear reactors—but also aspects of social planning and management. Machines will increasingly be in control of how we heat, light, and cool our cities and how we move around in them—and increasingly how we interact with local and national government. As increasing amounts of data about our actual behavior become available, it will be possible to automate decisions that affect our daily lives and the social behaviors we choose to encourage or discourage.

Transitioning from the automation and machine control we are already accustomed to, and dependent on, to a new level of control is only a small step. In this new level, machines are programmed to make decisions that were previously within the realm of policymakers or government messaging campaigns. The significant difference will be that data-driven decisions can be far more nuanced and effective than the typical "broad brushstroke" policies made by many policymakers.

A justice ministry, for example, is likely to be keen to reduce the reoffending rate for people convicted of an offense. As an increasing amount of data becomes available about people's behavior, it will be possible to see trends and patterns that reveal the kinds of personal circumstances and series of events that trigger reoffending.

Policymaking in the absence of such data and insight tends to be very blunt. A minister might, for example, decide to "send a message" about the seriousness of reoffending by being "tough on reoffenders" by sentencing convicted criminals who reoffend to ever harsher sentences. US President Bill Clinton, for example, signed a bill in 1994 that included the "three strikes and you're out" rule, which is phraseology taken from the game of baseball: anyone convicted of a serious violent crime who had two other convictions on their record—including nonviolent crimes, such as drug offenses—would receive a mandatory life sentence. Clinton later admitted the policy had contributed to overpopulated prisons and that a consequence has been that "we had a lot of people who were essentially locked up who were minor actors for far too long."[1] According to World Prison Brief, the United States has the highest prison population in the world, with over two million people, including those awaiting trial, imprisoned in 2019. This represents the world's highest incarceration rate of 629 per 100,000 national population.[2]

Automated policymaking is most likely to first appear at the level of local government. It used to be the job of town planners and local government officials to decide where and when people could park their cars, how much they should pay for their parking at different times, whether they should pay a charge to enter cities at a certain time, and what maximum speed limit should apply in different parts of the city. The automation of transport systems and the increasing use of self-driving cars will make all these policy and planning activities redundant as machines quickly ascertain which actions deliver the desired results.

Fully automated systems with self-driving cars will also be self-policing: it will simply not be possible to park in certain places, drive into certain parts of the city at certain

---

1 BBC, "Bill Clinton Regrets 'Three Strikes' Bill," BBC News, July 16, 2015, https://www.bbc.com/news/world-us-canada-33545971.
2 Helen Fair and Roy Walmsley, *World Prison Population List: Thirteenth Edition* (London: Institute for Crime and Justice Policy Research, 2022), 2, https://www.prisonstudies.org/sites/default/files/resources/downloads/world_prison_population_list_13th_edition.pdf.

times of day, or break various speed limits in force in designated areas. Where government officials currently urge citizens to consume less energy or water via messaging and imposing fines, it may soon become difficult for an individual citizen to, for example, use a hosepipe to water their lawn in a drought or run their air conditioning or central heating systems below or above a certain temperature. The government may automatically police various forms of antisocial behavior, with citizens facing automatic fines that are deducted from their bank balances if they are identified on camera dropping litter in public places or damaging public property.

Some will resist this level of automation on political or philosophical grounds, concerned this gives a "faceless state" too much power over its citizens. But the human faces used by states to enforce their laws are not always benign. Police officers can have prejudices against some sectors of society and be trigger-happy and local government officials corrupt. When applying for certain permits or licenses, it might be preferable to have a machine conduct the assessment instead of relying on an official who may suggest that "things would run more smoothly" or "we could overlook that fine" if a small personal payment was made.

A non-white citizen of the United States may prefer to be pulled over for a suspected traffic offense by a robot than by an armed policeman. The *New York Times* reported in 2021 that police officers in the United States had killed over four hundred drivers or passengers in the previous five years after stopping cars for suspected traffic offenses. None of the victims was armed or being pursued for a violent crime.³ A disproportionate number of Americans killed by police are Black or Hispanic. The *Washington Post* database of all fatal shootings indicates that police kill approximately one thousand civilians a year, with probability theory confirming that "the quantity of rare events in huge populations tends to remain stable absent major societal changes, such as a fundamental shift in police culture or extreme restrictions on gun ownership."⁴ There is another consistent factor in the data. Black Americans are more than twice as likely to be fatally shot by police than white Americans (6.1 per million per year for Black Americans versus 2.4 per million per year for white Americans).⁵

---

3   David D. Kirkpatrick et al., "Why Many Police Traffic Stops Turn Deadly," *The New York Times*, October 31, 2021, https://www.nytimes.com/2021/10/31/us/police-traffic-stops-killings.html.
4   Aaron Ross Coleman, "The Black Lives That Don't Make Headlines Still Matter," *Vox*, September 5, 2020, https://www.vox.com/2020/9/5/21423349/the-black-lives-that-dont-make-headlines-still-matter-dijon-kizzee-breonna-taylor.
5   "Police Shootings Database 2015–2024," *The Washington Post*, accessed April 23, 2024, https://www.washingtonpost.com/graphics/investigations/police-shootings-database/.

RoboCops are still in the realm of science fiction. A five-foot high (1.5 meter) robot in the shape of an artillery shell patrols a park in Huntingdon Park in southeast Los Angeles County. It has the word "POLICE" emblazoned on its blue and white casing and is officially known as the HP ("Huntingdon Park") RoboCop. The machine wanders along its pre-programmed route, humming a futuristic tune and pausing occasionally to say, "Please keep the park clean." The RoboCop's makers, a Silicon Valley company called Knightscope, describe their machines, which use self-driving technology and artificial intelligence, as "crime-fighting autonomous data machines"—though an *NBC News* report describes it as "little more than a glorified security camera on wheels." Meanwhile, a woman who saw a fight break out in the park rushed up to the robot and pushed its emergency alert button, hoping for a police response. The RoboCop did nothing other than to say, "Step out of the way" as its emergency alert button had not yet been connected to the police department and merely sent a message back to Knightscope instead. The chief of police confirmed to NBC that "It's a new program for us and we're still developing some protocols...to be able to fully develop the program."

Nonetheless, we can confidently expect that similar robots could soon be fully integrated with emergency services and play a significant role in how cities are policed. The

NBC report noted that the RoboCop seemed to be reducing crime in the immediate vicinity of its route—perhaps because potential criminals were uncertain of its capabilities. Park users who were not intent on criminality also found the RoboCop's presence reassuring. "A lot of people like it because they feel secure," a man who ran a concession stand in the park told NBC News.[6]

The increasing use of automation—and even automata (abstract self-propelled computing systems)—in devising and policing public policy is difficult new territory. Nobody has all the answers about how humans will interact with this technology and what unintended consequences there may be, but it is time to start the debate. As in so many other areas, it will become increasingly possible and increasingly *preferable* for aspects of our lives to be administered by machines, and for the machines—provided they are given clear and transparent parameters by human beings—to make decisions previously made by policymakers having various biases and political agendas who often based their decisions on incomplete data and a false understanding of people's real experiences.

---

6   Katie Flaherty, "A Robo Cop, a Park and a Fight: How Expectations about Robots Are Clashing with Reality," NBC News, October 4, 2019, https://www.nbcnews.com/tech/tech-news/robocop-park-fight-how-expectations-about-robots-are-clashing-reality-n1059671.

IT'S NOT ALWAYS SMOOTH SAILING

Surrendering control of human affairs to machines will not be plain sailing. To fuel the debate, let's examine some things that have gone wrong with early experiments in which machines were given control over aspects of human lives.

In the United Kingdom, the social distancing measures implemented in 2020 during the COVID-19 pandemic prevented the usual conduct of school examinations. There was concern that bringing large groups of students together in examination halls under the supervision of adults would encourage the spread of the virus.

The grades that students achieve in these annual examinations have a significant effect on their future lives, including the jobs they are offered, their continued educational path, and the universities that will accept them.

One way of awarding grades to students in the absence of examinations would have been to rely on teachers' assessments of students' performance. Their teachers routinely assessed all students in the United Kingdom based on their course work to date and their performance in the classroom, information which predicts the grades a teacher believes they will achieve on examinations. One option in 2020 was for the examining bodies to accept these teachers' predictions as being the best estimate of what a student would achieve under exam conditions. But there was concern that teachers might paint a rosy picture of their students' potential grades because the government's Department of Education grades schools based on various measures of the school's performance, including the exam grades achieved by its students.

In June 2020, England's exam regulator, Ofqual, used an algorithm to remove concerns about teacher-led grade inflation and to award fair and unbiased grades to students in the absence of examinations. Intentions were good; the algorithm was not.

Teachers were asked to supply two pieces of information about each student: their predicted final examination grades and their ranking in relation to other students predicted to get the same grade. The ranking would allow the algorithm to make decisions about whether someone near the top of the rankings predicted to get, say, a B grade in a particular subject should be moved up to an A grade, and whether some students at the bottom of the rankings should be moved down to a C grade, and so on.

So far, so good. It was a third factor programmed into the algorithm that caused the problems. Since the Department of Education grades all schools in the United Kingdom, the algorithm was programmed to take every school's performance over the past three years into account. A school seen to be performing badly would see its predicted grade levels downgraded so that if a poorly performing school predicted that certain students would earn A grades, the algorithm downweighed the prediction because it assumed a school's performance rating would be passed on directly to individual students. The result was that gifted and hard-working students in schools rated as performing poorly across the board were denied the grades they would almost certainly have achieved. The algorithm's calculations resulted in 36 percent of students across the country being given grades one ranking lower than their teachers' predictions, with 3 percent of students downgraded by two grades, and 79 percent of students destined for university not awarded their predicted grades—potentially denying them entry to the university of their choice.

To add insult to injury, the algorithm accepted the student grades predicted by teachers in high-performing schools and elite private schools—sometimes, grades were even enhanced. The algorithm assessed students studying in classes with fewer fellow students as being more likely to achieve the teachers' predicted grades. But smaller class sizes are a luxury affordable only in private schools, which saw the biggest increase in awarded A grades compared with the previous year.

The effects of the algorithm's calculations outraged and alarmed students, teachers, and parents. In August 2020, the government announced that the algorithm's results would be abandoned and grades would be awarded to reflect teachers' original predictions. The government's education secretary apologized for the "significant inconsistencies" in the algorithm's conclusions and acknowledged the distress it had caused.[7]

Another attempt to introduce algorithms in an educational context resulted in a high-profile 2014 lawsuit for the Houston Independent School District in Texas. In this case, the school district introduced an algorithm to evaluate the performance of teachers.

The creators set up the model, the Educational Value-Added Assessment System (EVAAS), to link students' scores in standardized tests to individual teachers. They aimed to calculate the impact each teacher had on their students' academic performance, measuring how much value the teachers added to their education. The algorithm delivered an assessment of teachers' effectiveness: well above, above, no detectable difference, below, and well below. If a teacher's

---

7 Camilla Turner, Anna Mikhailova, and Catherine Neilan, "Teachers Accused of Submitting 'Implausibly High' Predicted Grades as A-level Results Row Grows," *The Telegraph*, August 13, 2020, https://www.telegraph.co.uk/news/2020/08/13/teachers-accused-submitting-implausibly-high-predicted-grades/; "A-Levels and GCSEs: How Did the Exam Algorithm Work?," BBC, August 20, 2020, https://www.bbc.com/news/explainers-53807730.

rating was not deemed high enough, they could be fired. A private software company devised the algorithm called SAS and licensed it by the school district.

Teachers complained that their effectiveness was being affected by students' test results in subjects the teachers did not themselves teach, and that factors outside the teachers' control—such as students' socioeconomic backgrounds and their English language skills—were not taken into account.

Another major concern was the lack of transparency in which the algorithm was deployed. SAS deemed its algorithm to be a trade secret, which meant the whole system was an effective "black box" that could not be examined or questioned. Throughout its use, teachers could never see how their scores were being calculated. Teachers who were dismissed because of their EVAAS assessment were denied access to the statistics or modeling that led to their dismissal. A lawsuit filed by the Houston Federation of Teachers and six individual teachers argued that the system had deprived teachers of their constitutional right to due process. They argued that the lack of information about the system's calculations deprived them of their right to challenge a termination based on an EVAAS score. As the law and technology website *Atlas Lab* reported, "there was no rational relationship between EVAAS scores and the Houston Independent School District's goal of employing effective teachers" and that the system did not give teachers any information that would allow them to improve their performance to achieve higher ratings and avoid getting sacked.[8]

In October 2017, the court ordered the school district to pay $237,000 in legal fees and to cease using "unverifiable" value-added scores. The district ended its contract with SAS. One of the plaintiffs told *EducationWeek*, "I have always been devoted to my students and proud of my teaching skills. Houston needs a well-developed system that properly evaluates teachers, provides good feedback and ensures that educators will receive continuous, targeted professional development to improve their performance."[9]

These two examples are more salutary than alarming. Both failed because they relied on over-simplistic measures, such as "a school's previous performance will affect individual students' predicted achievements" and "student grades are the key measure of teachers' abilities." And the second example had the added twist of a lack of transparency. It is

---

8   Ching-Fu Lin, "Sorting Teachers Out: Automated Performance Scoring and the Limit of Algorithmic Governance in the Education Sector," in *Money, Power, and AI: Automated Banks and Automated States*, eds. Zofia Bednarz and Monika Zalnieriute (Cambridge: Cambridge University Press, 2023), 189–204, https://doi.org/10.1017/9781009334297.015.

9   Liana Loewus, "Houston District Settles Lawsuit with Teachers' Union Over Value-Added Scores," *EducationWeek*, October 26, 2017, https://www.edweek.org/teaching-learning/houston-district-settles-lawsuit-with-teachers-union-over-value-added-scores/2017/10.

clearly unacceptable for someone's career to end via black box technology that cannot be questioned or examined. The Houston teachers' point—that this lack of transparency takes away people's right to understand what they are seen to be doing wrong and to choose to do something about it—is fundamental.

But it is entirely possible to imagine other, more intelligent, systems that might have considered far more data and made more interesting and useful assessments. An automated system that can process a large amount of data about an individual student's academic record should be able to predict, with considerable accuracy, the grade the student is likely to achieve on future examinations. It is equally possible to believe that such a system would make a more accurate assessment than a busy, distracted teacher. Similarly, it is possible to imagine a machine that used many data points to assess a teacher's or any professional's performance and give a very accurate account of their abilities—whereas the simplistic EVAAS system relied on one measure alone: students' grades.

Another recent example of an attempt to introduce automation to a public service, this time in employment, shows how worryingly easy it is for data-based models to perpetuate existing market distortions. It also shows how machine-driven results can be distorted by the aims of the people designing the model so that what is presented as an "objective" decision made by disinterested machines is, in fact, a reflection of the interests of the model's designers.

In 2016, the *Arbeitsmarktservice* (AMS) in Austria ("Work Market Service" or Public Employment Service) tried using machines to help people find work. An algorithm profiled jobseekers and put them into one of three categories. The algorithm categorized job seekers into three groups, with Group A consisting of people who were assessed to have a more than a 66 percent chance of finding a position in the next seven months. This group received very little support, as resources were scarce and it was assumed they could manage without assistance. Group B consisted of jobseekers with a middling chance of success, a subset assumed to offer the best return on investment in terms of time and money spent helping them find a job. People assigned to Group C were assessed as having a less than 25 percent chance of finding employment in the next two years and, like Group A, this group was given little support because they were "lost causes" who would deliver a poor return on investment.

The technology used statistical models based on existing employment records to determine which factors were the best predictors of somebody's chances of finding a position. The models indicated that women had lower employment rates compared to men, so being female was considered to negatively affect a job seeker's chances of reentering the labor market. The same was true for disabled people and those over the age of thirty. People's "obligations of care," which came with a negative weighting, were applied to women alone. It was clear that the technology was deeply biased. An article published by *Frontiers in Big Data* highlighted issues that echo the Houston school district case:

> Criticism pointed to a lack of transparency, missing possibilities to remedy decisions for AMS customers, the use of sensitive information, possible unintended consequences, such as discrimination, misinterpretation and stigmatization, as well as its potential for reinforcing and amplifying inequality on the labor market. In particular, the inclusion of gender as a variable raised public concerns about gender discrimination.[10]

AMS argued that the system's results simply mirrored the "harsh reality" of the labor market. But using statistical models to create policy based on existing patterns of human behavior is a good example of what is known as the "is-ought problem" in moral philosophy. The fact that something *is* the

---

10   Doris Allhutter et al., "Algorithmic Profiling of Job Seekers in Austria: How Austerity Politics Are Made Effective," *Frontiers in Big Data* 3, no. 5 (February 2020), https://doi.org/10.3389/fdata.2020.00005.

case does not mean that it necessarily *ought* to be the case. Using a statistical model to reveal that fewer women, disabled people, or older people are currently employed should not—clearly—be allowed to dictate future policy.

The *Frontiers in Big Data* article also highlighted how the system's professed "*objectivity* and *precision*" was in practice colored by the drive for "the *efficiency* of public employment bureaucracies and the need for *effective* resource allocation" [original italics].[11] What was being presented as scientifically objective, machine-based analysis was actually being driven by particular managerial objectives. This is to a degree unavoidable, but it again highlights how essential it is to see what those managerial objectives are (for example, cost savings, and overall efficiencies) and not be hoodwinked by black box technologies whose core assumptions cannot be interrogated into believing that the judgments being made are completely objective and unbiased.

Here is another attempt to use machines to save money and improve efficiency in public services that also ultimately backfired. Between 2013 and 2015, 40,000 people in Michigan were wrongly accused of unemployment fraud by a flawed algorithm. Called the Michigan Integrated Data Automated System (MiDAS), which sounds very reassuring,

---

11　Allhutter et al., "Algorithmic Profiling," 2.

the algorithm did not, in fact, have the magical powers of the mythical king of Greek mythology who was granted his wish that everything he touched would turn to gold. When the mythical Midas realized this included turning his food and drink and not just the twigs and roses he had previously magically and happily converted into gold, he cursed his new power. The state of Michigan may feel the same way. The MiDAS system eventually cost it over $20 million in refunds after a group of private vendors had been paid $47 million to develop the system.

MiDAS was designed to determine unemployment eligibility, track case files, and reveal cases of fraudulent benefit claims. It worked marvelously, uncovering nearly 27,000 cases of supposed fraud in 2014, "more than five times the typical number," according to a report by *Time* magazine.

The system was programmed to intercept tax refunds for people who would normally be entitled to them but who were judged by the system to have made fraudulent claims. The state also seized millions of dollars of current wages of residents also deemed to have made previous fraudulent claims. The state routinely rejected victims' complaints of unfair treatment, even when it could not provide evidence to support the accusations of fraud made by the MiDAS system.

One couple, expecting their first child, received notification that they had been fined $10,000 for claims made after the husband had lost his job as a chef. In the three years that followed, their tax refunds were seized, their vehicle repossessed and, eventually, they were forced to file for bankruptcy—even after the state reversed its charges and repaid the couple $6,000, which went straight to pay their lawyers' fees. In 2020, the couple's previous bankruptcy meant they were still unable to take out a mortgage or rent an apartment for themselves without a cosigner. "It just makes you feel like a lesser person," the wife told *Time* magazine.[12]

Before implementing this software, the state faced financial difficulties. Unemployment levels were high and incomes were worryingly low compared to the rest of the United States. When the Great Recession struck in 2008, things got worse. Michigan cut more than $3 billion in state spending between 2007 and 2011. The Unemployment Insurance Agency alone owed the federal government $3.8 billion. The contract with private developers to develop MiDAS was a desperate attempt to save and recover money. But government officials' understanding of the technology was minimal and the state had little say in how the system was built or worked.

A partner at Fast Enterprises—one of the companies responsible for the software's development—defended the

---

12 Alejandro De La Garza, "States' Automated Systems Are Trapping Citizens in Bureaucratic Nightmares with Their Lives on the Line," *Time*, May 28, 2020, https://time.com/5840609/algorithm-unemployment/.

technology, arguing that it was not the company's responsibility to interpret the law. He also argued that the state's persistence in using the flawed judgments proved they were not flawed, telling *Time* magazine that "had the system been wrong it would have been fixed right away. I think that's pretty good evidence it was never wrong, because it was well known what was happening and it was still decided to keep doing it."[13] Which is effectively like saying, "We could all see this miscarriage of justice unfolding before our eyes, but nobody did anything about it—which I think proves that it wasn't a miscarriage of justice after all."

On the subject of miscarriages of justice, the United Kingdom is still in the middle of what has been described as "the greatest miscarriage of justice ever in the history of the UK," which began when the country's Post Office installed new accounting software, *Horizon*, in all its branches.[14] The software was fraught with various issues, and also suggested that money was missing from individual branch office accounts when, in fact, it was not. Rather than consider it was more likely the software was faulty, rather than over seven hundred branch managers suddenly turning to a life of crime,

---

13 Garza, "States' Automated Systems."
14 Karen Peattie, "Entrepreneur Calls Post Office Scandal 'Greatest Miscarriage of Justice in UK History,'" *The Herald*, May 1, 2022, https://www.heraldscotland.com/business_hq/20105400.entrepreneur-calls-post-office-scandal-greatest-miscarriage-justice-uk-history/.

the post office used its powers to bring criminal prosecutions. The reputations of subpostmasters and postmistresses in their local communities were destroyed and, in some cases, people were imprisoned.[15] There were suicides and divorces.

If we are going to use machines in sensitive areas of human business—as we increasingly will and must—we must guard against blind faith in their capabilities. Computer anomalies are a fact of life, programmers make errors, and statistical data reflects existing biases and injustices. These are issues that must be faced and addressed, not ignored. It is perfectly possible to give machines safe and effective governance of human affairs, but only if all parties understand the aims and intents of the program—and only if there is transparency and a fast and efficient system of feedback and redress that accepts that a new machine-driven program is not infallible and citizens who believe they are being unfairly treated may be telling the simple truth. In some of today's most advanced AI platforms, there are always safety and ethical concerns for language models to go into incorrect tangents. AI models today are not immune from their own issues, not least of which include *hallucinations*, when an AI model continues to generate incorrect or misleading results.

---

15 "Post Office Horizon Scandal: Why Hundreds Were Wrongly Prosecuted," BBC, May 24, 2024, https://www.bbc.com/news/business-56718036.

THE PROBLEM OF BIAS

Facial recognition technology offers another example of how bias—unconscious or otherwise—can creep into automated systems. Once the stuff of science fiction, the technology is fast becoming commonplace. We encounter it when opening some smartphones, going through border checkpoints at airports, and applying for new bank cards. In recent years, law enforcement surveillance has also begun using this technology. Police departments all over the world run images of suspects through photographic databases and for "predictive policing" initiatives. But studies of its effectiveness suggest that—much as with Austria's AMS algorithm—it can be inherently flawed and can reinforce existing discriminatory biases.

A report by the Georgetown Law Center on Privacy and Technology in 2016 estimated that nearly half of all American adults have been affected by law enforcement requests to run searches against databases of driver's licenses and ID photos. The report estimates that 117 million Americans appear on law enforcement face recognition networks—about 36 percent of the US population in 2016. The report makes the point that use by the FBI to build a biometric network from driver's license photos means the vast majority of images on the database are of law-abiding citizens, whereas "historically,

FBI fingerprint and DNA databases have been primarily or exclusively made up of information from *criminal* arrests or investigations [original italics]."[16] A face recognition search of people who have been legally stopped or arrested is different, the report argues, from images collected from the driver's license database or people walking past surveillance cameras. "The former is targeted and public," the report says. "The latter are generalized and invisible."[17]

There is another problem. Because Black Americans are more likely to be arrested and incarcerated for minor crimes than white Americans, their photographs are overrepresented in these databases, creating an ingrained bias that encourages further surveillance and suspicion of Black citizens. In cities, including Boston and San Francisco, the dangerous potential of facial recognition software has already been identified and police and local agencies have been banned from using it.[18] This inbuilt bias has the potential to infringe on individuals' rights, including privacy, freedom of expression, and freedom of association. People may choose

---

16 Clare Garvie, Alvaro Bedoya, and Jonathan Frankle, "Perpetual Line Up: Unregulated Police Face Recognition in America," Georgetown Law Center on Privacy & Technology, October 18, 2016, https://www.perpetuallineup.org/.
17 Garvie, Bedoya, and Frankle, "Perpetual Line Up."
18 Ally Jarmanning, "Boston Bans Use of Facial Recognition Technology: It's the 2nd-Largest City to Do So," WBUR, June 24, 2020, https://www.wbur.org/news/2020/06/23/boston-facial-recognition-ban.

not to protest in public, for example, for fear that their images will be captured and used against them in some way in the future.

Using facial recognition technology is further complicated by its accuracy. Studies suggest recognition is generally more than 90 percent accurate, but the technology is often used in ways that assume it is 100 percent accurate. Results have also been shown to vary greatly depending on ethnicity and gender. In 2018, the Gender Shades project considered three gender classification algorithms, including one designed by IBM and another by Microsoft. Subjects were grouped into four categories: darker-skinned females, darker-skinned males, lighter-skinned females, and lighter-skinned males. The results were unanimous; all three algorithms performed worst on darker-skinned females, with error rates 34 percent higher for these women than for lighter-skinned males. Both IBM and Microsoft responded positively, promising to change their testing cohorts and alter their approach to data collection. Algorithms would be trained on more diverse datasets, cameras would be better adapted to capture darker skin tones, and independent sources would carry auditing out to verify the effectiveness and fairness of the technology.

A second Gender Shades audit tested Amazon's Rekognition software, a cloud-based computer vision platform based on machine learning that Amazon has sold to several US government agencies and corporations. As with earlier findings, it was found to have high error rates for darker-skinned women.[19]

While these are examples of bias and error creeping unintentionally into automated systems, there is also concern about the use of social media data (and, potentially, facial recognition technologies) to discriminate intentionally against certain groups of citizens. In 2019, the US Department of Housing and Urban Development sued Facebook for allowing property advertisers to select who would see their advertising based on users' race, religion, or country of origin. "Using a computer to limit a person's housing choices can be just as discriminatory as slamming a door in someone's face," said Housing Secretary Ben Carson in announcing the lawsuit.[20]

In 2019, US senators Cory Booker and Ron Wyden and Representative Yvette D. Clarke introduced the Algorithmic Accountability Act, empowering the Federal Trade Commission to require companies to investigate automated decision

---

19 Alex Najibi, "Racial Discrimination in Face Recognition Technology," *Science in the News* (blog), Harvard Kenneth C. Griffin Graduate School of Arts and Sciences, October 24, 2020, https://sitn.hms.harvard.edu/flash/2020/racial-discrimination-in-face-recognition-technology/.
20 Katie Benner, Glenn Thrush, and Mike Isaac, "Facebook Engages in Housing Discrimination with Its Ad Practices, U.S. Says," *The New York Times*, March 28, 2019, https://www.nytimes.com/2019/03/28/us/politics/facebook-housing-discrimination.html.

systems and training data to assess their impact on "accuracy, fairness, bias, discrimination, privacy, and security."[21] Introducing the Act, Senator Booker recalled an earlier era of housing discrimination in America:

> 50 years ago my parents encountered a practice called "real estate steering," where black couples were steered away from certain neighborhoods in New Jersey...the discrimination that my family faced in 1969 can be significantly harder to detect in 2019: houses that you never know are for sale, job opportunities that never present themselves, and financing that you never become aware of—all due to biased algorithms.[22]

The intentional use of facial recognition to target people based on ethnicity becomes even more sinister when used by nation-states. China has faced growing criticism for its treatment of the majority-Muslim Uighur population. The Uighurs are a Turkic ethnic group, originating in Central and

---

21 "Proposed Algorithmic Accountability Act Targets Bias in Artificial Intelligence," Jones Day, June 2019, https://www.jonesday.com/en/insights/2019/06/proposed-algorithmic-accountability-act.

22 Office of US Senator Cory Booker, "Booker, Wyden, Clarke Introduce Bill Requiring Companies to Target Bias in Corporate Algorithms," press release, April 10, 2019, https://www.booker.senate.gov/news/press/booker-wyden-clarke-introduce-bill-requiring-companies-to-target-bias-in-corporate-algorithms.

Eastern Asia, and their homeland is in the Xinjiang autonomous region of the People's Republic of China in the country's northwest. The Chinese government has reportedly detained more than a million Uighurs in internment camps, citing concerns about "extremism," "separatism," and "international terrorism."[23]

In 2019, *The New York Times* reported on the existence of facial recognition technology that used the country's growing system of surveillance cameras to identify Uighurs living in other regions of China and track their movements. As an associate at the Center on Privacy and Technology at Georgetown Law told the *Times*, "If you make a technology that can classify people by ethnicity, someone will use it to repress that ethnicity."[24]

Any technology that has the potential for good can also have the potential for evil. Using algorithms, machine learning, facial recognition, and all other forms of machine intelligence in human society carries risks—as does the use of any machine—but the risks all lie in the design and

---

23 Lindsay Maizland, "China's Repression of Uyghurs in Xinjiang," Council on Foreign Relations, September 22, 2022, https://www.cfr.org/backgrounder/china-xinjiang-uyghurs-muslims-repression-genocide-human-rights.
24 Paul Mozur, "One Month, 500,000 Face Scans: How China Is Using A.I. to Profile a Minority," *The New York Times*, April 14, 2019, https://www.nytimes.com/2019/04/14/technology/china-surveillance-artificial-intelligence-racial-profiling.html.

implementation of the technology and the moral choices made that underlie its use.

The Tony Blair Institute for Global Change argues in a 2018 white paper entitled "Public Artificial Intelligence: A Crash Course for Politicians and Policy Professionals" that the use of AI "promises a radical transformation of public-service delivery, allowing governments to meet each citizen's needs, freeing up time for civil servants and front-line staff, and putting data at the heart of decision-making," while also acknowledging the technology's "potentially disruptive economic and social impact."[25]

The Institute identifies four policy domains for the use of AI, classified according to their potential impact and feasibility:

- High-feasibility and high-impact domains, including healthcare, welfare, energy, and the environment.
- High-feasibility, low-impact areas (which it describes as "no regrets" domains because they have no apparent downside), including tax, pensions, and licensing.

---

25 Limor Gultchin, "Public Artificial Intelligence: A Crash Course for Politicians and Policy Professionals," Tony Blair Institute for Global Change, November 6, 2018, https://www.institute.global/insights/tech-and-digitalisation/public-artificial-intelligence-crash-course-politicians-and-policy-professionals.

- Low-feasibility domains with potentially high impact (which the report calls "investment areas"), including transport, education, and foreign policy.
- Low-feasibility and low-impact domains, including (in the report's opinion) housing, emergency services, and regulation.[26]

The report calls for governments to make better use of the data at their disposal to deliver improved services, but also calls on them to take responsibility for ethics, fairness, and transparency. Perhaps most importantly, the report calls for the creation of "a vibrant ecosystem of research, industry and government bodies" to "shape AI development in the public interest."[27]

LEARNING TO USE OUR CLEVER TOOLS

New technologies can be both marvelous and confusing. We struggle to fit them into the existing framework of our ideas. My great-uncle was the person responsible for first introducing movies to what is now the United Arab Emirates. His first venture was a traveling cinema; he would tour the

---

26 Gultchin, "Public Artificial Intelligence."
27 Gultchin, "Public Artificial Intelligence."

region with a screen and a projector and put on shows. But some tribal leaders refused to allow him to show his films because they regarded the technology as "sorcery."

One allowed my great-uncle to show his film: an Egyptian-made saga about a great Arab leader. My great-uncle's host was so entranced that he asked him to stay on and show the film again to guests who were arriving the following day. The second showing was also a great success. The leaders' guests marveled at the technology that allowed them to witness historic events and the exploits of the famous hero—as if they were unfolding before their very eyes. But the leader was apologetic. "You should have seen him last night," he said to his guests, talking about the man playing the hero on screen as if he was a real actor performing in real time. "He was better yesterday; I think he must have been tired after that performance."

What seems miraculous today will be commonplace tomorrow. We will increasingly use digital technologies to help us devise and implement policy, run our cities more efficiently, and police our citizens. There will be teething problems; mistakes will be made. Bad algorithms will be written, and conscious and unconscious biases will creep in. We will use these technologies for good and for ill.

But they are just technologies, clever tools. In the blink of an eye, they have the capacity to process volumes of data that we can barely comprehend, and this gives them the ability to see patterns and trends and make decisions regarding certain desired goals far better than humans. They will adjust to such decisions in real time as the data changes. And they will not be prone to various human failings and obscure motivations that can make our policymaking and its enforcement so flawed.

CHAPTER 9

SINGAPORE
BUILDING A NATION FROM SCRATCH

F WE ARE GOING TO USE DIGITAL TECHNOLOGIES TO help provide policy kits to emerging nations and help all governments with implementing policy, we need to have a clear idea of what we mean by "policy."

In developed nations, policy looks overwhelmingly complicated—too "messy" and altogether too "human" to be meaningfully automated—but the Republic of Singapore offers a near-perfect example of how policy can transform a nation. Singapore first came to prominence as an important British trading station between East and West in the nineteenth century. It suffered great damage when it was invaded by Japanese forces during World War II. The island gained independence from Britain in 1959 and later declared unilateral independence, becoming part of the new state of Malaysia, alongside the former Federation of Malaya and the former British Crown colonies of North Borneo and Sarawak. When Singapore was ejected from Malaysia, for reasons covered shortly, it faced a deeply uncertain future. Other than its well-situated port, the island had almost no natural resources. The fact that this tiny nation-state became one of the four Asian Tiger economies, alongside South Korea, Taiwan, and Hong Kong, seems a little short of miraculous, but it is not a miracle. It is the result of intelligent policies effectively implemented.

Before exploring those policies in more detail, it is worth noting Singapore's remarkable history in a little more detail to realize the desperate situation faced by Singapore when, in 1965, it first became an independent nation-state.

The island of Singapore was acquired in 1819 by Britain's East India Company, the quasi-governmental trading organization of the British Empire, from a Malayan Sultan. The initiator of this transaction was Sir Thomas Stamford Bingley Raffles, who could see the island's potential as a major entrepot trading post. In the days of wind-powered ships, entrepot ports and cities played an important role in facilitating global commerce by making available suppliers, warehousing goods, and enabling the journey of goods to their final destinations. Singapore, then as now, was perfectly placed to facilitate east-west trade, situated as it is on the Strait of Malacca, a narrow sea passage between the tip of the Malaysian peninsula and the Indonesian island of Sumatra. The Strait offers the shortest sea route between India and the Middle East to the west, and the Philippines, China, Japan, and Korea to the east. Singapore was also a perfect place to refit and resupply the British merchant fleet, offering the East India Company a useful outpost from which to try to check the advances of its great rival, the Dutch East India Company.

When Raffles signed a treaty with Singapore's previous ruler, the island had around one thousand inhabitants, mostly Orang Laut, though a few dozen Malayan and Chinese traders had also settled there.[1] Fishing was the main occupation outside of the port and trade-related activities. There were also plantations of gambier, a plant that yields an extract that can be used as gum for chewing slices of betel nut, a stimulant, an ancient and common practice in Southeast Asia.

Singapore would later become part of the British territories in Southeast Asia known as the Straits Settlements, which also included several Malayan territories, that was

---

1   "1819 Singapore Treaty," National Library Board Singapore, last modified May 15, 2014, https://www.nlb.gov.sg/main/article-detail?cmsuuid=92bb56f0-e821-40d1-bd8c-cf8fa7e7f172.

governed by the British Raj in India. In 1867, the Straits Settlements came under the direct control of Britain and Singapore became a Crown Colony. The island's population had by then grown to some eighty thousand, over 60 percent of whom were Chinese immigrants attracted by Singapore's growing prosperity. The development of rubber plantations in British Malaya and Singapore itself in the late nineteenth century made Singapore a world center for the sorting and export of rubber. After World War I, Britain built a huge naval base at Sembawang on the northern tip of the island as part of its strategy to deter potential aggression from the Empire of Japan. The base included what was the world's largest dry dock and the world's third-largest floating dock. It had enough fuel tanks to supply the entire British Navy for six months.[2]

Britain's "Singapore Strategy" for containing Japanese naval aggression didn't work very well. One day after the Japanese attack on Pearl Harbor on December 7, 1941, a British naval squadron sailed out of Singapore to intercept a Japanese fleet launching an amphibious attack on Malaya. The British task force, which had sailed with no air cover, failed to intercept the Japanese fleet. Having lost the element of surprise, the attack was canceled. The force was returning

---

2 David Hobbs, *The British Pacific Fleet: The Royal Navy's Most Powerful Strike Force* (Annapolis, MD: Naval Institute Press, 2015), 5.

to Singapore when it was attacked by a Japanese submarine that fired five torpedoes—all of which missed. The British forces were not even aware they had been attacked. But the submarine signaled their position back to Japanese headquarters. Land-based bombers and torpedo bombers were dispatched and the battleship HMS *Prince of Wales* and battlecruiser HMS *Repulse* were both sunk—the first time in history an air attack had sunk a major warship on the high seas.

The Japanese amphibious assault on Thailand and northern Malaya was successful, with Japanese troops quickly moving south through Malaya using bicycles confiscated from locals on plantation roads and local paths—a maneuver the British had discounted as impossible because of Malaya's supposedly impassable jungle terrain. Hastily organized defenses in Malaya were either outflanked or overrun. The British destroyed the causeway between the mainland and the island of Singapore, but the Japanese established a beachhead after crossing the Johore Strait at night in barges and collapsible boats and overwhelming the Australian defenders.

Singapore was defended by 85,000 Allied troops—predominantly Australian and Indian with some British and local volunteers—most of whom lacked experience and with few defensive positions set up. Most of Singapore's water supplies came from the Malayan mainland. The Japanese, who by then had achieved air supremacy in the region, bombed water supplies on the island, where around one million civilians were now gathered. On February 15, 1942, one week after the first Japanese soldiers had crossed the Johor Strait, British Lieutenant-General Arthur Percival capitulated. About eighty thousand Allied troops became prisoners of war, joining some fifty thousand troops captured in Malaya. British Prime Minister Winston Churchill had at first wanted the defenders of Singapore to fight to the death. He wrote to Archibald Wavell, commander-in-chief of British forces in India, saying, "There must at this stage be no thought of saving the troops or sparing the population. The battle must be fought to the bitter end at all costs...The honour of the British Empire and of the British Army is at stake."[3] After Percival's surrender—which Churchill finally authorized, having realized that further resistance was suicidal—Churchill called the defeat the "worst disaster and largest capitulation in British history."[4]

The British Empire's projection of power in the region was dealt a fatal blow. The Empire was no longer seen as invincible, and its permanence in the region was no longer inevitable.

---

3   Wikipedia, s.v. "Fall of Singapore," last modified July 6, 2024, https://en.wikipedia.org/wiki/Fall_of_Singapore.
4   Ronnie McCrum, "Singapore, February 1942: The Worst Disaster and Largest Capitulation in British History," *Military History*, The Past, March 16, 2012, https://the-past.com/feature/singapore-february-1942-the-worst-disaster-and-largest-capitulation-in-british-history/.

It was the beginning of the end of an era. The one thing no one would have predicted at the time was the restructuring of power and influence in what Europeans thought of as the "Far East" and that Singapore—an island roughly four times the size of Washington, DC—would rise to global prominence.

How was this possible? There are several reasons, but the core was that the government of a newly independent Singapore—following its forced separation from the Federation of Malaya—adopted a series of enlightened and highly effective policies that transformed the economy of the new city-state. My intention is not so much to hold up Singaporean policies as a paradigm for all developing nations to follow—though there are certainly worse paradigms—but to highlight that this coherent set of policies can be readily identified. It would be entirely possible to codify the core policies that have led to Singapore's dramatic economic growth and stable society. Many heads of state have sought to learn its secrets—including President Paul Kagame of Rwanda, who said in 2013 after his advisors had visited on a fact-finding mission: "We are not seeking to become Singapore but we can be like Singapore. We must have a vision of where we want to go and work harder...to achieve it."[5] According to

---

5 Edwin Musoni, "President Kagame Calls for Increased Efforts to Devt," *The New Times*, January 13, 2013, https://www.newtimes.co.rw/article/86535/National/president-kagame-calls-for-increased-efforts-to-devt.

Rwanda's daily newspaper *The New Times*, in the same speech, Kagame mentioned recent cuts in development aid from the West and commented, "Dependency takes away our dignity and leaves behind an empty shell; the lesson is that we must double our efforts to achieve more than we had projected. In this context, we cannot afford to walk, we must run."[6]

New technologies—and the emergence of AI in particular—will mean that governments no longer need to visit foreign states to learn the secrets of their success. It will be possible to offer the governments of developing nations a selection of policy kits, available "off the shelf," that can deliver a framework of policy options. With these core frameworks in place, it will also be possible to plug in essential data on each nation's citizens and infrastructure to flesh out that framework with real numbers, using AI to calculate optimal budget levels, carry out ongoing evaluation, and make automatic adjustments for the most effective implementation of those policies.

STARTING FROM SQUARE ONE

Singapore emerged from the Japanese occupation with almost nothing. It was dependent on the Malay mainland

---

6   Musoni, "President Kagame Calls."

for most of its water, had very little land for agriculture, and no oil or mineral wealth. The Japanese occupation had been brutal, especially for Chinese Singaporeans (due to Japan's war with China that predated World War II), who were singled out as being "anti-Japanese" and summarily executed in the Sook Ching Massacre. Meaning "purging and cleansing" in Chinese, "Sook Ching" was the Japanese Army directive, issued on February 18, 1942, ordering all Chinese males aged eighteen to fifty to report to screening centers. The directive was designed to apprehend political activists, members of anti-Japanese volunteer forces, communists, triad gangsters, and specific individuals on Japanese-maintained lists of hostiles. In practice, the Kempeitai (military police) and Imperial Guards Division who carried out the screenings and executions were more indiscriminate.

The Singapore government's website, HistorySG, reports that people wearing glasses or with soft hands were executed as being "educated" and therefore suspect. HistorySG also reports that though Japanese estimates of the numbers executed were in the region of five thousand to six thousand, local people put the number at between forty thousand and sixty thousand, though the website acknowledges some of these deaths may have been caused by bombardment during the Japanese assault on Singapore. Men singled out during the "screenings" were loaded onto lorries and taken into the countryside, where they were killed. Villagers and prisoners of war were ordered to dispose of the bodies.[7]

The British made plans for the recapture of Singapore but could not carry them out before the war ended, which led to an outbreak of looting and revenge killings. Food was scarce, leading to rice rationing and bread lines. Destruction of housing by bombardment and air attack had caused serious overcrowding, with thousands living in shanty towns. Malnutrition and disease led to death rates of twice pre-war levels.[8] Historian John Curtis Perry describes the post-war island in his book, *Singapore, Unlikely Power*:

> Malaria raged and cases of tuberculosis rose. Most households lived in one room; many in overcrowded and rundown quarters, some with open bucket toilets shared by many families and cooking done over charcoal fires…Spawned by the occupation, lawlessness prevailed. Prostitution, crime and corruption ran rampant, the traditional vices of opium smoking and gambling flourished, and wildcat strikes erupted frequently. Racial

---

[7] Stephanie Ho, "Operation Sook Ching Is Carried Out," National Library Board Singapore, accessed July 7, 2024, https://www.nlb.gov.sg/main/article-detail?cmsuuid=cc4da337-3bcd-4f96-bdc6-5210646bdd90.

[8] Barbara Leitch LePoer, "Aftermath of War: 1945–55," in *Singapore: A Country Study*, ed. Barbara Leitch LePoer (Washington, DC: U.S. Library of Congress, 1991), 41–42.

tensions simmered, threatening to break into violence. At the great base of Sembawang, the large floating dock lay on the bottom of the sea with a sunken ship clasped in its embrace.⁹

The British Military Administration took over Singapore after the Japanese surrender and did not cover itself with glory, establishing links to corrupt officials and profiteers who had flourished during the Japanese occupation. The management and distribution of rice was so inefficient and inequitable that locals lampooned them as the "Black Market Administration." When military rule ended in 1946, gas, water, and electricity had been restored and the port returned to civilian control, though it was not fully functional until 1951.

Worldwide demand for rubber and tin helped the economy recover. Singapore was a modest producer of rubber but a significant hub for the processing and exporting of both rubber and tin from Malaya and Indonesia. The Korean War (1950–1953) pushed demand for these commodities even higher and the Singapore economy saw something of a boom, though the 1950s were turbulent years, with civil unrest linked to the communist-led insurgency in Malaya

---

9 John Curtis Perry, *Singapore: Unlikely Power* (Oxford: Oxford University Press, 2017), 147–148.

against British rule (known as the Malaya Emergency). The People's Republic of China, founded in 1949 by the Chinese Communist Party, meant there were many communist sympathizers in the region, particularly among ethnic Chinese. The insurgency in Malaya was put down by the British with considerable violence. The emergency was declared over in 1960, though further communist insurgency flared up again some years later and did not fully end until the Malayan Communist Party signed a peace accord with the Malaysian government in 1989.

Singapore made good use of its trading infrastructure—its docks, warehouses, banks, commodity markets, and specialized trading skills—and traded in other goods, though rubber was still predominant as Singapore had become the world's biggest rubber market. By the mid-1950s, Singapore's volume of trade exceeded pre-war levels.[10]

In 1959, Britain granted Singapore autonomy in all areas of government, apart from foreign affairs and defense. A new political group, the People's Action Party (PAP), won power in the subsequent elections under the leadership of Lee Kuan Yew and pressed for greater independence. The Federation of Malaya had become independent of Britain in 1957. In 1963, Lee declared the unilateral independence of Singapore from

---

10 Perry, *Singapore: Unlikely Power*, 151–153.

British rule and announced that Singapore would become part of the newly founded state of Malaysia.

Singapore and Malaysia made uneasy bedfellows. The peninsular region of Malaysia was predominantly Malay, but with a sizable ethnic Chinese population. Ethnic Malayans were nervous about Singapore's majority ethnic Chinese population. The addition of Singapore to Malaysia added a significant proportion of ethnic Chinese to the new federation, with the Malay population fearing it would become outnumbered. Despite an agreement that the political parties in Singapore and the Malaysian peninsular would stay off each other's territory, the dominant political party in Malaysia fielded candidates in Singapore in 1963, especially in areas with a Malay population. They were unsuccessful, but the PAP then felt free to field candidates on the Malay peninsula in 1964. Though they won only one seat, this was seen as a blow to the Malaysian party's prestige and led to concerns that the Singaporean PAP might make further inroads on the peninsula. An anti-PAP campaign in Singapore aimed at Singapore's Malay population led to increased tensions between Malays and ethnic Chinese on the island, leading to race riots. There were fears of ethnic tensions spreading to the Malaysian peninsula. Underlying these racial tensions, there was a fear of a communist insurrection in Singapore, led by the considerable number of communist sympathizers among Singaporean

Chinese, which could spark another communist insurgency on the peninsula. In 1965, the Malaysian Parliament voted unanimously to expel Singapore from Malaysia.

Singapore, against its wishes, had become an independent republic. It needed to import nearly all its food and raw materials and even most of its water. It needed roads, housing, schools, and jobs. Plus, it had lost access to the Malaysian market and, therefore, urgently needed to open other markets around the world. There was also the imperative to calm racial tensions and forge a new Singaporean identity that transcended ethnicity while ending the threat of a communist takeover. Above all, it needed foreign investment, which meant convincing the outside world that Singapore was a place to do business. Prime Minister Lee Kuan Yew wrote of his fears for the future in his memoirs:

> We had been asked to leave Malaysia and go our own way with no signposts to our next destination. We faced tremendous odds with an improbable chance of survival. [...] On that 9th day of August 1965, I started out with great trepidation on a journey along an unmarked road to an unknown destination.[11]

---

11 Jon S. T. Quah, "Why Singapore Works: Five Secrets of Singapore's Success," *Public Administration and Policy* 21, no. 11 (2018): 5, https://doi.org/10.1108/PAP-06-2018-002.

SINGAPORE RISES

Faced with the sudden prospect of being alone in the world with few resources to fall back on, Singapore achieved a truly astonishing societal and economic transformation over the course of the coming decades. It did this through a series of well-thought-through policy decisions designed to address the major issues facing the new republic: the rooting out of corruption, establishment of political stability, rapid economic development, and the provisioning of housing, social welfare, education, information infrastructure, and transportation. The scale of these tasks was daunting. But the new nation-state's first priority was to create jobs.

Soon after Singapore was granted internal self-governance in 1959, the United Nations Development Programme team organized a visit to explore options for industrialization and other forms of development. It was led by Albert Winsemius, a Dutch national who worked at the country's Ministry of Finance as director-general of industrial development, responsible for the rebuilding of Dutch industry after the devastation of World War II. Winsemius served as an economic advisor to the government of Singapore for the next two decades and was hugely influential in creating its development strategy.

Winsemius saw the continuing potential of Singapore's port, having witnessed the rebuilding of the Dutch port of Rotterdam after its near destruction to its subsequent emergence as Europe's leading seaport. Singapore, situated halfway between the oil producers of the Middle East and the emerging markets of the East, was perfectly placed. The United States invented the shipping container in the 1950s, and Winsemius quickly grasped its potential. The fact that containers were prepacked at the point of origin and remained unopened until they reached their destination removed the previous work of unloading goods from incoming cargo ships and sorting them before shipping them to the next stage in their journey. Winsemius urged Singapore to adapt its port to take advantage of the coming container revolution, which would dramatically reduce shipping costs and contribute hugely to the post-war boom in international trade and globalization. He recommended the development of an ambitious new port and industrial center at Jurong on the island's south coast, where an area of mangrove swamps, rivers, fishponds, and plantations was filled and leveled to create usable land. Within three years, Jurong was home to around fifty enterprises that created over five thousand jobs.[12]

---

12 Perry, *Singapore: Unlikely Power*, 180.

The new Jurong Shipyard established a joint venture with Japan's Ishikawajima-Harima Heavy Industries. The fact that their new Japanese partner had not been involved in the Japanese war effort made the alliance more palatable to Singaporeans, though it was also an indication of the new republic's pragmatism and determination not to bear grudges about its colonial past or wartime experiences. Over the years, Singapore developed a range of increasingly sophisticated maritime services, from ship breaking to ship building, ship repair, oil rig construction, and oil tanker servicing. The Shell Refining Company opened the island's first oil refinery at Pulau Bukom in 1961.[13] Mobil, British Petroleum, and Esso soon followed suit.[14] Today, the US International Trade Administration reports that "Singapore has become one of the most important shipping centers in Asia and is often listed as one of the world's top three oil trading and refining hubs."[15]

Beyond the industries that serviced its port, during the years it was part of Malaysia, Singapore had focused on labor-intensive industries such as clothing, furniture, and

---

13 "Shell Opens Singapore's First Oil Refinery at Pulau Bukom," National Library Board Singapore, accessed April 23, 2024, https://www.nlb.gov.sg/main/article-detail?cmsuuid=37c6a7dd-c7de-4378-819e-e2407839f8d5.
14 "Esso's Refinery Opens at Pulau Ayer Chawan," National Library Board Singapore, accessed April 23, 2024, https://www.nlb.gov.sg/main/article-detail?cmsuuid=5e547f82-ef3b-489b-8a2a-79ece9f14cea.
15 "Energy Resource Guide," International Trade Association, accessed April 23, 2024, https://www.trade.gov/energy-resource-guide-singapore-oil-and-gas.

hardware. This was the policy of "import substitution" common to many developing nations—the decision to prioritize the production of home goods that would otherwise have needed to be imported from other countries. These industries created jobs and average wages in Singapore were high compared to the region. After its ejection from Malaysia, and loss of that "home" market, such goods were not competitive in the international market; the multinational corporations that Singapore was keen to attract had no interest in manufacturing them. Singapore's Economic Development Board (EDB), set up in 1961 with the Israeli economist E. J. Mayer as its first managing director, set out to attract more high-tech and knowledge-based industries.

Winsemius reached out to Dutch multinational Philips, persuading them to set up an operation in Singapore or "miss the boat in the growing market of Southeast Asia."[16] Philips already had a small team in Singapore, established in 1951, that managed the distribution of imported Philips products. In 1968, they set up a manufacturing plant at Boon Keng Road, and in 1970, they opened a second plant at the Jurong Industrial Estate.

In 1969, Texas Instruments opened a semiconductor manufacturing plant employing 1,400 workers, mainly women.

---

16 Perry, *Singapore: Unlikely Power*, 183.

Singapore had impressively demonstrated its eagerness to attract such foreign investment and prioritized making such developments happen quickly. Texas Instruments opened their Singapore facility in November 1968, and production began in January 1969:

> Last November the board of directors of Texas Instruments Inc. decided in Dallas to set up a factory in Singapore to manufacture electronic components.
>
> Within the month—on November 20—an initial start-up team left Dallas from Singapore.
>
> Last month Texas Instruments' Kallang Basin factory was in production. This month regular batches of Singapore made semi-conductors and integrated circuits began flowing back to the United States.
>
> Corporate decision to product delivery took only three months. And the time taken to physically implement the project was seven weeks—just under 50 days.[17]

Hewlett Packard (HP) followed suit in 1970, leasing the top two floors of a government building. In this instance, Singapore could demonstrate not only its speed of operation but also its

---

17 Ivy Siow, "50 Day Wonder," *The Straits Times*, February 23, 1969, 1, https://eresources.nlb.gov.sg/newspapers/Digitised/Article/straitstimes19690223-1.2.4.

spirit of can-do ingenuity. A transformer was under order to supply power to the floors that HP would occupy, but it did not arrive in time for a visit by HP's founder, William Hewlett. No power meant no working escalator and the all-important Mr. Hewlett having to walk up six flights of stairs to look at his new premises. Singapore's Economic Development Board strung a large cable from a nearby building to supply power, which allowed Mr. Hewlett to ride the escalator and turn on the lights.[18]

If Singapore was speedy and ingenious in setting up new facilities for foreign investors, it was also persistent in its salesmanship. In his book *Strategic Pragmatism: The Culture of Singapore's Economic Development Board*, Edgar Schein of the MIT Sloan School of Management quoted from a 1993 interview of his with HP executive Clyde Coombs. Coombs had been tasked with finding whether it was viable for the company to manufacture their core-memory components rather than buy them from other manufacturers, including finding countries with lower labor costs but a sufficiently skilled labor force to cope with the precise, though repetitive, tasks involved in manufacture:

> I identified thirteen possible countries and after investigating formal materials, boiled things down to Taiwan,

---

[18] Perry, *Singapore: Unlikely Power*, 183–184.

Japan, Hong Kong, and Singapore. Taiwan was an early favorite, but was eliminated because it looked like there were too many political problems, too many rules, and potentially too much graft and corruption. Japan was not seriously considered at this point because of labor costs. Hong Kong looked feasible for short-run investments but, because of potential future political instability vis-à-vis the People's Republic of China, it would not be a good place for a long-range investment. So things began to point to Singapore.

I then telephoned Eric Goh, who headed the San Francisco office of the EDB. The minute I told him what we were thinking about, he was all over me; he was really a salesman who just wouldn't quit. If I needed any information he would get it immediately, and he just wouldn't give up until we had at least agreed to visit Singapore and see for ourselves.[19]

By 1973, HP had 1,800 employees and, according to the HP Computer Museum, it was "the fastest growing HP entity ever."[20] Early foreign investors in Singapore were rewarded

---

19 Edgar H. Schein, *Strategic Pragmatism: The Culture of Singapore's Economic Development Board* (Cambridge, MA: The MIT Press, 1997), 19.
20 "HP Singapore," HP Computer Museum, accessed April 23, 2024, https://www.hpmuseum.net/divisions.php?did=24.

with "pioneer status," giving them largely tax-free operations for several years. Shell had been the very first "pioneer" corporation after building their refinery on Pulau Bukom Island and became the proud recipient of Pioneer Certificate No. 1.[21]

---

21 Serene Loo, "Shell AS Singapore's Pioneer Certificate No.1 Investor, Kicks Off EDB's 50th Anniversary Heritage Relay," Shell Media, January 18, 2011, https://www.shell.com.sg/media/2011-media-releases/singapores-pioneer.html.

CHAPTER 10

THE POWER OF POLICY

SINGAPORE HAD TAKEN STEPS TO CONSOLIDATE ITS position as a leading trading hub, begun the move into shipbuilding and other maritime services, geared up for the coming shipping container revolution, and brought in foreign investors who created new skilled jobs. They had pivoted away from their previous key trading partners of Malaysia and Indonesia and toward a truly global market. Having created a lifeline with the potential to pull its citizens into a more affluent future, Singapore enacted a remarkable series of core policies that would help turn the young republic into a developed nation.

CONTROL OF CORRUPTION

During the Japanese occupation of Singapore, corruption had become endemic. The scarcity of food and every other commodity led to a thriving black market in which civil servants, who could barely survive on their wages in a time of rampant inflation, became complicit.

Things did not greatly improve with the resumption of British rule. The sparsely staffed Anti-Corruption Branch was part of the Singapore Police Force, requiring the Force to police its own behavior with unsurprising results. In 1951, thieves stole a large shipment of impounded opium from a police depot. A subsequent investigation revealed the involvement of several high-ranking police officers. The embarrassing event led to the creation of the Corrupt Practices Investigation Bureau (CPIB).[1]

When limited self-governance was granted to Singapore in 1959, the PAP won the subsequent general election with a landslide victory. In his memoirs, the PAP's longtime leader said:

---

1. Zeger van der Wal, "Singapore's Corrupt Practices Investigations Bureau: Guardian of Public Integrity," in *Guardians of Public Value*, eds. Arjen Boin, Lauren A. Fahy, and Paul 't Hart (Cham, Switzerland: Palgrave Macmillan, 2021), 64, https://doi.org/10.1007/978-3-030-51701-4_3.

We were sickened by the greed, corruption and decadence of many Asian leaders. We had a deep sense of mission to establish a clean and effective government. When we took the oath of office in June 1959, we all wore white shirts and white slacks to symbolize purity and honesty in our personal behavior and our public life. We made sure from the day we took office in June 1959, that every dollar in revenue would be properly accounted for and would reach the beneficiaries at the grass roots as one dollar, without being siphoned off along the way.[2]

The Singapore government enhanced the legal powers, staffing, and financial resources of the CPIB and made it independent of the governing party. Under the jurisdiction of the Prime Minister's office, the director of the CPIB reports to the secretary of the cabinet—a civil servant—and can obtain the consent of the elected president to investigate ministers, members of parliament, and senior civil servants over the head of the prime minister. The CPIB takes a zero-tolerance approach to major or minor corruption, regardless of the rank, status, or influence of the people involved. Bribe givers and takers are seen as being equally culpable. The CPIB has

---

2 van der Wal, "Singapore's Corrupt Practices," 63.

successfully prosecuted several PAP leaders and senior civil servants over the years.[3]

Singapore raised the salaries for public servants, with three aims: remove the incentive for corruption, prevent an exodus of talent to the private sector (which became a significant issue in the 1970s when private sector salaries increased as the economy improved), and ensure that Singapore's civil service would continue to attract its brightest and best young people. After a succession of pay increases that closed the gap between public and private sector salaries, in 1994, the government put a permanent solution in place by pegging the salaries of ministers and senior civil servants to an average of the salaries of the four highest-paid executives in six private sector professions: accounting, banking, engineering, law, local manufacturers, and multinational corporations operating in Singapore. The government white paper "Competitive Salaries for Competent and Honest Government" defended the measure as essential for maintaining "an efficient public service and a competent and honest political leadership, which have been vital to Singapore's prosperity and success."[4]

---

[3] van der Wal, "Singapore's Corrupt Practices," 63–86.
[4] Office of the Prime Minister of Singapore, *White Paper on Competitive Salaries for Competent & Honest Government: Benchmarks for Ministers & Senior Public Officers*, Cmd. 13 of 1994 (Singapore: The Prime Minister's Office, 1994), 18, https://www.nas.gov.sg/archivesonline/government_records/record-details/a0bef428-730e-11e7-83df-0050568939ad.

With those exceptional benefits, however, came exceptional responsibilities and restraints. As Kent E. Calder of the John Hopkins School of Advanced International Studies and Edwin O. Reischauer Centre for East Asian Studies wrote in *Singapore: Smart City, Smart State*, "Singaporean civil servants operate under extremely severe behavioral constraints and reporting requirements."[5] The officers of today's CPIB all take the following pledge:

> We, the officers of the CPIB, pledge to be loyal to the Republic of Singapore and the Bureau.
>
> We pledge to uphold our values of integrity, teamwork and devotion to duty.
>
> We pledge to combat corruption through swift and sure, firm but fair action; and to uphold good governance to make Singapore a corruption-free nation.[6]

In 2021, the World Bank Worldwide Governance Indicators awarded Singapore a score of 2.14 on a scale of −2.5 to +2.5 for Control of Corruption, placing Singapore third in world rankings, behind only Denmark (2.33) and Finland (2.24).[7]

---

5 Kent E. Calder, *Singapore: Smart City, Smart State* (Washington, DC: Brookings Institution, 2016), 44.
6 "The CPIB Pledge," Corrupt Practices Investigation Bureau, accessed April 23, 2024, https://www.cpib.gov.sg/who-we-are/our-corporate-philosophy/pledge.
7 "Worldwide Governance Indicators," World Bank Group, accessed April 23,...

STATUTORY BOARDS

Singapore's statutory bodies are especially significant in this book because they perform the function that I argue could, to a large extent, be filled by artificial intelligence, especially in developing nations lacking ministerial know-how and well-educated and experienced civil servants. Calder described the statutory boards as...

> ...autonomous agencies of government established by acts of parliament and overseen by government ministries. They are not staffed by civil servants, so have somewhat more operational flexibility and frequently broader technical expertise than the ministries. They also draw in many employees as well as some directors from the private sector, enhancing the sensitivity of the boards to broad market trends.
>
> The boards thus give the working-level officials that lead them a clear, specific mandate for action, allowing those officials to sidestep the cross-ministerial bureaucratic politics that often complicate implementation elsewhere in the world. The boards also shield operating

---

...2024, https://www.worldbank.org/en/publication/worldwide-governance-indicators#home.

officials from the political accountability prevailing in ministries themselves, rendering bureaucratic action in Singapore unusually technocratic and impervious to politically inspired and budget-busting patronage politics. The statutory boards have the added final merit of devolving policy decisions to small organizations with clear oversight responsibilities, giving such bodies the ability to take quick and effective action when needed.[8]

Calder's point about the statutory boards being "unusually... impervious to politically inspired and budget-busting patronage politics" harks back to the earlier point about the near inevitably of "pork-barrel spending" in any political system where representatives of different geographical constituencies control spending budgets. Statutory boards take this kind of deeply inefficient but endemic political behavior out of the equation, allowing for highly efficient and effective targeted action that is not distorted by the usual political horse-trading.

Calder draws attention to other key benefits of the statutory board system, including an efficient organizational structure, high caliber staff, and "predictable regulatory parameters, especially the rule of law."[9] His description of the

---

8 Calder, *Singapore: Smart City*, 41–42.
9 Calder, *Singapore: Smart City*, 43.

Statutory Boards as "unusually technocratic" supports the argument that the boards are a good role model for a kind of automated, AI-empowered "virtual government agencies" that this book envisages.

THE ECONOMIC DEVELOPMENT BOARD

When Singapore's Economic Development Board (EDB) was set up in 1961, it was given a budget of S$100 million (around $1.4 million at 1961 exchange rates). According to *Singapore Infopedia*, a Singaporean government agency website, the aims of the EDB were to:

> investigate and evaluate new industrial opportunities; provide financial assistance or guarantee loans; participate in establishing new industries; and lay out industrial sites with power, water and other facilities. It was also responsible for sourcing overseas technical experts, as well as making expert personnel, capital, technical services and market research available to local manufacturers and existing industries.[10]

---

10 Puay Ling Lim, "State Development Plan, 1961–1964," National Library Board Singapore, October 10, 2017, https://www.nlb.gov.sg/main/article-detail?cmsuuid=00df90f2-a3ac-4e9b-b507-f338eb2f933c.

Singapore's GDP grew from around $705 million in 1960 to $1.92 billion in 1970, $11.9 billion in 1980, $36.14 billion in 1990, $96.08 billion in 2000, $239.81 billion in 2010, and just over $500 billion in 2023.[11] This places Singapore in the top forty of the world's nations by GDP, ahead of Hong Kong and Vietnam. Its 2022 per capita GDP of $88,428 is even more astonishing—eleventh in the world. Many countries outranking Singapore in per capita GDP are also tax havens rather than wealth producers: Liechtenstein, Luxembourg, Bermuda, the Isle of Man, the Cayman Islands, and Monaco, for example. The other four countries that outperformed Singapore in terms of per capita GDP in the 2022 data were Ireland, Switzerland, Norway, and Qatar.[12]

Today, Singapore's EDB says the industries it has helped set up in the republic account for more than one-third of its GDP. The board actively helps already-established companies boost productivity and transform their businesses in "adjacent and disruptive areas" and says it works closely with other Singaporean agencies to "constantly improve our pro-business environment."[13]

---

11 "GDP (Current US$)—Singapore: 1960–2023," World Bank Group, accessed April 23, 2024, https://data.worldbank.org/indicator/NY.GDP.MKTP.CD?locations=SG.
12 "GDP per Capita (Current US$)—Singapore: 1960–2023," World Bank Group, accessed April 23, 2024, https://data.worldbank.org/indicator/NY.GDP.PCAP.CD?locations=SG&most_recent_value_desc=true.
13 "Who We Are," EDB Singapore, accessed April 23, 2024, https://www.edb.gov.sg/en/about-edb/who-we-are.html.

According to World Bank data, from 2016 to 2019, Singapore ranked second to New Zealand in "Ease of Doing Business," with Hong Kong, Denmark, and South Korea rounding out the top five.[14] Singapore ranked seventh among one hundred nations worldwide in StartupBlink's Startup Ecosystem Index 2022, which measured the best locations for startups, behind only the United States, the United Kingdom, Israel, Canada, Sweden, and Germany—making it the highest ranking Asia-Pacific nation. The report cited Singapore's favorable tax environment and ease of doing business as reasons for its high ranking.[15]

THE HOUSING DEVELOPMENT BOARD (HDB)

The Housing Development Board (HDB) was established in 1960 to replace the Singapore Improvement Trust (SIT), which had struggled with the immense problems caused by a growing population and the destruction caused by the Battle of Singapore and the subsequent Japanese occupation.

---

14 "Ease of Doing Business Score (0 = Lowest Performance to 100 = Best Performance)—Singapore: 2015–2019," World Bank Group, accessed April 23, 2024, https://data.worldbank.org/indicator/IC.BUS.DFRN.XQ?most_recent_value_desc=true.

15 Rei Kurohi, "S'pore Tops Asia-Pacific in Ranking for Start-Ups, 7th in the World," *The Straits Times*, June 11, 2022, https://www.straitstimes.com/business/spore-tops-asia-pacific-in-ranking-for-start-ups-7th-in-the-world.

Construction of new public housing was slow and further delayed by a sclerotic bureaucracy. As the *The Straits Times* reported in September 1958:

> The Trust [SIT] has been waiting eleven months for approval for a $38 million programme of nearly 7,000 houses and shops. The Trust also has in view two New Town schemes at Toa Payoh and Woodlands to house between them 100,000 people. These sites, and others, will require a great deal of clearance work before development can begin…Already the delay in approving the $38 million programme has put progress back by several months.[16]

The *Straits Times* also reported the more fundamental problem the SIT had in providing housing that was affordable:

> The rents of most of the post-war property and all the pre-war flats are still uneconomic…The Trust has been letting for $30 and $35 a month flats which would carry an economic rent of $60. And the Trust has been unable to build anything for the cubicle dweller who cannot afford $30 a month.[17]

---

16 "The Housing Problem," *The Straits Times*, September 12, 1958, 8, https://eresources.nlb.gov.sg/newspapers/digitised/article/straitstimes19580912-1.2.105.1.
17 "The Housing Problem," *The Straits Times*, 8.

SIT building was subsidized by government loans. The cost of clearance of sites and the deficit in the public housing account caused by fixing rents at affordable levels was also met by the government.

The new HDB took up the challenge, announcing a program to create nearly 53,000 housing units over five years at a cost of $230 million in 1960.[18] Land was acquired, slums were torn down. A fire in a squatter settlement in 1961 left nearly sixteen thousand people homeless.[19] After an impressive emergency relief program, flats were quickly constructed in an existing 1920s-era SIT housing estate in the central region of Singapore. The fire site was subsequently obtained by the government for further low-cost housing development. The derelict inner-city tenements and the shanty towns that had sprung up on the city's edge disappeared. Inhabitants of primitive Malay *kampongs* (villages) were rehoused in the new high-rise estates, each with an infrastructure of shops, schools, and clinics. New public transport systems linked the new estates with each other and with central Singapore.

---

18 "Govt. to Spend $230 Mil. on Homes in Next Five Years," *The Straits Times*, August 10, 1960, 4, https://eresources.nlb.gov.sg/newspapers/digitised/article/straitstimes19600810-1.2.32.

19 "Bukit Ho Swee Fire Occurs," National Library Board Singapore, accessed April 23, 2024, https://www.nlb.gov.sg/main/article-detail?cmsuuid=a67e0450-c429-49b2-b87c-fb1a26105f4b.

The HDB had embarked on a program not only to supply good quality and affordable public housing but also to bring about social engineering. Tension among the republic's three main ethnic groups—Chinese, Malay, and Indian—had always been high. As the housing program developed into the 1980s and 1990s, it became clear that ethnic groups were concentrating in certain enclaves, raising fears of renewed ethnic conflict. In 1989, the government introduced a system of quotas limiting the proportion of ethnic Chinese, Malay, or Indian residents in apartment buildings and neighborhoods.

This attempt to encourage racial integration applied only to new developments. Given the attractiveness of the public housing on offer, it was a sugar-coated pill most people were happy to swallow in return for access to new, high-quality homes and amenities. The results were impressive. The stabilizing effect of home ownership and the fact that people of all ethnicities with different levels of income were mixing socially—living in the same apartment blocks, sharing the same amenities, and with their children attending the same schools—forged a new sense of being "Singaporean." Everyone came together to share the visible benefits of the young republic's growing success.

As one Singaporean politician, Tharman Shanmugaratnam (a Singaporean senior minister since 2019) said in 2015, when he was deputy prime minister:

If we believe in social inclusion, if we believe in opportunities for all, we have to accept it doesn't happen automatically because of the invisible hand of the market or the invisible hand of society. It happens because you've got policies that seek to foster and encourage it.[20]

Shanmugaratnam also described the quota policy as the most intrusive—but also the most effective—way to integrate Singapore's multiethnic society.

Early HDB homes were simple and utilitarian, designed to be quick to build. Over time, they became more modern and stylish. Accommodation was provided for not only nuclear families but also single people, the elderly, and multigenerational families. Shared spaces around the estates were improved with landscaping and additional recreational facilities. Kindergartens and community halls were built.

By the end of the 1970s, over one-third of Singaporeans were living in an HDB home; by 1989, the percentage had risen to over 80 percent.[21] Early homes had been offered for

---

20 Beatrice Weder di Mauro, *Building a Cohesive Society: The Case of Singapore's Housing Policies: Policy Brief No. 128* (Waterloo, ON: Centre for International Governance Innovation, April 2018), 1–2, https://www.cigionline.org/publications/building-cohesive-society-case-singapores-housing-policies/.

21 Singapore Infopedia, "Housing and Development Board," National Library...

rental only, but in 1964, a home ownership plan was introduced. Today, around 90 percent of the population owns their own home.[22] Early owners could sell their homes back to the HDB five years after buying them, and after 1971, owners were allowed to sell them on the private market, which led to a robust secondary property market that has turned Singaporeans' homes into substantial assets.

In a 2018 report for the Centre for International Governance Innovation, *Building a Cohesive Society: The Case for Singapore's Housing Policies*, the author cites different sources showing that 75 percent of the retirement wealth of a typical Singaporean worker over fifty is the value of their home, compared to 20 percent for a typical US household. The HDB has introduced various schemes to enable people to release this home equity to support their retirement, with cash bonuses for elderly owners who choose to downsize and free up their homes for new owners.[23] Rental properties are available to citizens on low incomes who have no other housing options.

...Board Singapore, November 2023, https://www.nlb.gov.sg/main/article-detail?cmsuuid=3abd40aa-0d91-4352-b9fe-0de1d68e3d85.
22 "Singapore Home Ownership Rate," Trading Economics, accessed April 23, 2024, https://tradingeconomics.com/singapore/home-ownership-rate.
23 di Mauro, *Building a Cohesive Society*, 5.

EDUCATION

When Singapore gained independence from Britain in 1959, its population was predominantly illiterate and unskilled. With its remarkable focus on building a modern economy and a recognition that its only significant resources were its deep-water port and its people—its "human resource"—the government set about creating a modern education system from scratch. As a report for the OECD's Programme for International Student Assessment (PISA) states, the new education system would be "to deliver the human capital engine for economic growth and to create a sense of Singaporean identity."[24] The report divides the republic's efforts into three phases: "survival-driven" (1959–1978), "efficiency-driven" (1979–1996), and "ability-based, aspiration-driven" (1997 to the present). These three phases reflect Singapore's changing ambitions.

The first ambition was indeed survival. Singapore's goal to attract foreign investment for labor-intensive manufacturing suited to its low-skilled workforce. Over time, and when facing growing competition from other Asian countries for such low-cost, labor-intensive projects, Singapore

---

24 OECD, "Singapore: Rapid Improvement Followed by Strong Performance," in *Strong Performers and Successful Reformers in Education: Lessons from PISA for the United States* (Paris: OECD, 2011), 161, https://doi.org/10.1787/9789264096660-8-en.

sought to change to higher-skilled manufacturing and put a corresponding emphasis on providing young Singaporeans with more technical skills. More recently, Singapore identified its potential as part of the global knowledge economy, focused on delivering world-class research and innovation-led education, and partnering with leading universities around the world to focus on innovative technologies. The National University of Singapore (NUS) calls itself "a leading global university centered in Asia." The 2022 Times Higher Education World University Rankings ranked NUS twenty-first in the world and third in Asia, behind Tsinghua and Peking Universities in China but ahead of the University of Hong Kong, University of Tokyo, and Seoul National University. Singapore's Nanyang Technological University is ranked fourth in Asia.

The republic's "survival" phase was implementing the essentials of a basic education system and it was so effective that universal state-funded primary education was achieved in 1965 and universal lower secondary education by the early 1970s. Schools were rapidly built and teachers recruited. A special agency was formed to provide textbooks. Schools established by different ethnic groups were merged and there was a real determination to create a meritocratic, united society that was free from the interracial conflicts that had plagued Singapore. Every child was taught English—which would become the common language through which all teaching took place—and either Malay, Tamil, or Mandarin (though many ethnic Chinese Singaporeans spoke different Chinese dialects at home). English speakers were taught Malay; Malay and Tamil speakers were taught English; and Chinese students were taught Mandarin and English. Beginning in 1966, students made a daily pledge at school assemblies, facing the national flag:

> We, the citizens of Singapore, pledge ourselves as one united people, regardless of race, language or religion, to build a democratic society, based on justice and equality, so as to achieve happiness, prosperity and progress for our nation.[25]

With the fundamentals of an education system in place, there was a deliberate move to improve the quality of education. As the OECD's PISA report said of the education system at this time:

> In the early 1970s, out of every 1,000 pupils entering primary grade one, only 444 reached secondary grade

---

25 Singapore Infopedia, "National Pledge," National Library Board Singapore, August 1, 2014, https://www.nlb.gov.sg/main/article-detail?cmsuuid=ccc2229a-f8ec-4069-9feb-9b3e327a7bdf#.

four after 10 years. And of these, only 350 (35 percent of the cohort) gained three or more passes in O-level examinations. A significant report by Dutch economic advisor Dr. Albert Winsemius estimated that every year between 1970 and 1975, Singapore would be short of 500 engineers and 1,000 technical workers and would have a severe shortage of people with management skills.[26]

Uncharacteristically, there was a period of indecision, with several policy changes proving ineffective. Attempts to improve the perceived status of vocational education failed. Teacher morale was low, and many left the profession.

In 1979, at the beginning of Singapore's "efficiency-driven" phase, a key report written by the new Minister for Education Goh Keng Swee set the education system on a clear new path. Goh had already served as head of several other ministries and was also deputy prime minister from 1973 to 1985. The new focus was on providing many pathways through the education system for students of different interests and abilities, who could take more time to complete different stages of their education.

There were three types of high school: academic focused on preparing students for college and perhaps university,

---

26 OECD, "Singapore: Rapid Improvement," 161.

polytechnic delivering advanced occupational and technical training that could also lead to college entrance, and technical providing more basic occupational training. From 1992 onward, Singapore raised the status of blue-collar jobs many students were being trained to fill. It invested significantly in a new Institute for Technical Education (ITE), with several campuses offering high-quality facilities rivaling those of universities. Top ITE students could move on to polytechnics and universities. Vocational education became a meaningful, career-focused choice. Today, around one in four Singaporean students enroll with ITE, which the Ministry of Education describes as "one of the key components of Singapore's education system."[27] The move to streaming students into different pathways was unpopular at first, but dropout rates fell, and by 1986, only 6 percent of students left school with fewer than ten years' education.[28]

The education system's goal of "nurturing every child" led to offering additional learning support for students falling behind in core areas such as literacy and mathematics. Self-help community groups identify social conditions that are

---

27 "Structure of Education in Singapore," Singapore Education Guide, accessed April 23, 2024, https://www.singaporeeducation.info/education-system/structure-of-education.html.
28 OECD, "Singapore: Rapid Improvement," 162.

adversely affecting children's educational potential and provide a range of support measures, including financial help.[29]

The final, "ability-based, aspirational driven" phase of Singapore's developing education system involved a major pivot toward what the PISA report called "a paradigm shift... towards a focus on innovation, creativity and research."[30] There was less focus on learning by rote and more on giving students learning skills and encouraging their natural curiosity. School administration was taken away from a centralized, top-down system and given more autonomy within local "clusters" of schools. Cluster superintendents were appointed from the ranks of former successful school principals and charged with mentoring their colleagues and creating an atmosphere of innovation. With the additional autonomy came new forms of accountability. The old inspection system was transformed, with schools setting their own goals and assessing progress through a set of nine measures, four based on academic performance and five on how the school was delivering "enablers" to help students develop their learning skills. Major investments were made in information and communication technology for schools to give students the tools to explore self-directed learning.

---

29 OECD, "Singapore: Rapid Improvement," 165–167.
30 OECD, "Singapore: Rapid Improvement," 162.

They gave the new initiative the banner title, "Thinking School, Learning Nation." The new Agency for Science, Technology, and Research (known as A*Star) was created, mandated to build bridges between academia and industry while driving "mission-oriented research that advances scientific discovery and technological innovation" and to integrate research activities with the needs of multinational corporations, "globally competitive companies," and R&D-based startups the agency describes as "seeding for surprises and shaping for success."[31] It also provides research funding and sets out to attract top scientists and leading scientific companies to work in Singapore.

The National University of Singapore and Nanyang Technological Agency formed research partnerships with leading universities in other countries, and the National Research Foundation of Singapore made an ambitious linkup with MIT to form the Singapore–MIT Alliance for Research and Technology (SMART), MIT's first and only research center outside the United States to date.

The PISA report highlights the way Singapore's education system is driven by impressive levels of forward planning and constant evaluation of the effectiveness of its various

---

31 Agency for Science, Technology and Research: Singapore, "Our Mission & Vision," About A*STAR, accessed April 23, 2024, https://www.a-star.edu.sg/about-astar/overview.

policies. The Manpower Ministry works with the EDB and other agencies to forecast future skill requirements. The National Institute of Education (NIE), which handles all teacher training, ensures educators are equipped to deliver educational requirements set out in new policies. As noted in the PISA report, "[the system's] remarkable strength is that no policy is announced without a plan for building the capacity to meet it."[32]

Singapore has been particularly successful in teaching math and science. The country's primary education lasts for six years, starting around age seven. Teachers start teaching math from the first year of primary education and science from the third year. Both remain core subjects every student must take throughout secondary education, which lasts for four or five years and leads to the Singaporean General Certificate of Examination (GCE) O-Level exams. In the 2019 Trends in International Maths and Science Study (TIMSS), Singapore ranked top in math and science achievement at both grades four and eight (equivalent in Singapore to primary four and secondary two).[33] The country has ranked among the top countries for math and science achievement

---

32 OECD, "Singapore: Rapid Improvement," 166.
33 I. V. S. Mullis et al., *TIMSS 2019 International Results in Mathematics and Science* (Boston: IEA TIMSS & PIRLS International Study Center at Boston College, 2020), https://timss2019.org/reports/.

in every study, which occurs every four years since first administered in 1995.

CENTRAL PROVIDENT FUND

The British initially set up Singapore's Central Provident Fund (CPF) in 1955, with the intention, as Kent Calder writes in *Singapore: Smart City, Smart State* "to ensure that outlying parts of the empire did not burden the metropole unduly with their local social challenges."[34] It should help workers in their retirement without putting in place an expensive national pension scheme funded by Britain. However, Prime Minister Lee Kuan Yew's PAP party took it up after independence and transformed it into what the CPF itself today describes as "a key pillar of Singapore's social security system."[35]

The CPF is a system of compulsory savings for Singaporean workers and permanent residents. In 1968, the PAP extended its scope beyond the provision of retirement care to help people buy the public housing being built by the HDB. It was believed—correctly—that encouraging home ownership would give people a stake in Singaporean society. It was also expected that people would be helped in retirement, as they

---

34 Calder, *Singapore: Smart City*, 72.
35 Central Provident Fund Board, "How CPF Works," CPF Overview, accessed April 23, 2024, https://www.cpf.gov.sg/member/cpf-overview.

would own their homes by the time they reached retirement age and would no longer have to use their savings to pay rent.

All workers earning above a low threshold contribute automatically to their fund, supplemented by one from their employer. Contributions are higher for younger people and reduce as a person ages. Current contributions are 20 percent of wages for those under fifty-five, with employers contributing 17 percent of wages, so for every dollar saved by a worker, their employer contributes eighty-five cents to their fund. For those aged fifty-five to sixty, both parties contribute 14 percent. Contributions fall to 8.5 percent for workers aged sixty to sixty-five and 10 percent for the employer, with further reductions for older workers. The CPF Board invests the savings in special government bonds, which pay the same rate of interest received by contributors. The board includes members from government, employed federations, and trade unions to ensure the interests of all stakeholders are represented.

In the 1980s, they introduced a Special Account to supplement what then became known as the Ordinary Account. The authorities encourage savers not to use all their Ordinary Account savings for a house purchase—either as a cash purchase or to help service payments for a housing loan—and to hold some money back for retirement. The Special Account dedicates savings to funding people's lives after they stop working.

The government introduced a new MediSave Account (MA) was also introduced in the '80s to help people save for medical treatment or hospitalization. The government provides subsidies that make basic healthcare affordable, with further subsidies depending on income and the level of service a patient chooses. There are five tiers of healthcare service, ranging from the luxurious to the basic. Choosing the top class of treatment means paying for everything, while choosing the lowest class means the government will pay up to 80 percent of the cost. The end result, according to a 2017 article in the *New York Times*, is that one-third of healthcare spending in Singapore is paid by the government and two-thirds by private individuals, which the article points out is "just about the opposite [to] in the United States."[36] World Bank data for 2022 shows that Singapore's spending on healthcare represented about 6 percent of GDP, as opposed to almost 17 percent for the United States and around 13 percent for Germany and France.[37] The article also points out

---

36 Aaron E. Carroll and Austin Frakt, "What Makes Singapore's Health Care So Cheap," *The New York Times*, October 2, 2017, https://www.nytimes.com/2017/10/02/upshot/what-makes-singapores-health-care-so-cheap.html.

37 "Current Health Expenditure (% of GDP)—Singapore, United States, Germany, Netherlands, Japan, France, Australia, Korea, Rep.," World Bank Group, data retrieved April 15, 2024, https://data.worldbank.org/indicator/SH.XPD.CHEX.GD.ZS?locations=SG-US-DE-NL-JP-FR-AU-KR&year_high_desc=true.

that life expectancy in Singapore is "two to three years longer than in Britain or the United States" and infant mortality rates are among the lowest in the world, "about half that of the United States, and just over half that of Britain, Australia, Canada, and France."[38]

Contributions to the MA increases with age as the need for medical care increases. Savings may also buy yearly premiums in approved insurance plans that cover potential large healthcare bills and the provision of care for the disabled and people needing long-term help.

Singaporeans are now required to have a minimum level of savings in their Special Account and MA by the time they reach fifty-five years of age. Once that minimum is reached, savers can withdraw the remaining CPF funds in full or on demand. At sixty-five, it is possible to use savings to buy an annuity with the national insurance scheme, CPF Life, which will provide a guaranteed income for life. Savers can also use their Ordinary and Special Account savings to make investments in a range of approved schemes once their savings have reached a certain level.[39]

---

38 Carroll and Frakt, "What Makes Singapore's Health."
39 Central Provident Fund Board, "Investing Your Savings with CPF Investment Schemes," Growing Your Savings, accessed April 23, 2024, https://www.cpf.gov.sg/member/growing-your-savings/earning-higher-returns/investing-your-cpf-savings.

The CPF has far-reaching ramifications for Singaporean society. Encouraging top levels of home ownership has helped create a stable political environment and given most citizens a stake in society. Rising property values have meant that people's leases on their homes have become a significant asset that helps to fund their retirement.

The compulsory savings approach represented by the CPF also engenders a sense of self-reliance. Singaporeans appreciate the fact their savings "pot" is their own money, rather than a nominal share in some national scheme. It also avoids redistribution: the "rich" are not required to pay for the "poor." Their substantial contributions to the costs of their healthcare create an awareness of the actual costs involved and reduce the sense of entitlement to any treatment, regardless of cost, which comes with health systems that promise "free" comprehensive healthcare for all. By opting for a policy of defined contributions rather than defined benefits, Singapore has avoided the problems encountered by many developed nations, where guarantees of certain levels of benefits in terms of pension, healthcare, and other social services have become increasingly, and perhaps unsustainably, expensive as populations live longer and the cost of increasingly sophisticated healthcare treatments rises.

CLEAR-EYED POLICYMAKING

As stated earlier, we do not intend for the policies discussed above to be an exhaustive or definitive account of Singapore's policies. Other significant areas where Singapore has implemented effective and often innovative policies include taxation (free trade, low taxes), transport (affordable public transit, taxes and quotas that discourage car ownership, an electronic road-pricing system to deter drivers from entering heavily congested areas), food production (rooftop and vertical farms), and water supply (catchment, recycling, retreatment, desalination).

Policies in developed nations become messy. Different political parties have been tinkered with over many governments for so long, it is hard to discern their original intent or what clear actions were and are being taken. Taxation policy, for example, becomes so complex it is typically only possible to say that a particular government has been a tax-cutting or a tax-increasing government. Even when taxes decrease in one headline area—such as the basic rate of income tax—the total amount of taxes raised may well increase. Successive finance ministers tinker with the existing system to raise more money without being too obvious about it while pleasing various special interest groups, putting in place allowances, rebates, exemptions, and special circumstances that become so complex that even typical households may need to employ accountants to ensure they are not paying more tax than they are obliged to.

Most developed nations' housing policy is difficult to discern or describe. Governments usually encourage private house building while attempting to ensure the supply of affordable, "social" housing is adequate. Most developed nations still suffer from significant levels of homelessness and relative degrees of housing unaffordability. The education policy in most developed nations is a messy hotchpotch from generations of new initiatives reflecting the successive ideologies and priorities of various governments.

With Singapore, the situation is unique. This is partly due to the nation's youthfulness, but also because of the immense challenges it encountered. Moreover, the remarkable success of its implemented policies highlighted the entire process distinctly. In Singapore's case, the initial problems, and specific policies put in place to address them, along with the results, can be easily observed.

The core argument of this book has been that government policy is not, or need not be, the sole province of highly educated ministers and deeply experienced civil servants and bureaucrats. Policy, at heart, is simple. As we saw in the first chapter of this book, the purpose of policy is to create functional, successful societies—what the Sienese artist Ambrogio Lorenzetti portrayed as "The Virtues of Good Government." Headline policies are just high-level principles that set out clear goals; for example, to drive economic development, provide affordable housing, create an education system that gives people the skills and knowledge they need to take up well-paid employment, drive economic growth, and help people provide for their needs in old age. Implementing this headline policy is then just a set of if-then instructions—an algorithm—and the success of any policy's implementation can be easily measured by the progress achieved toward the desired goal.

Policymaking and implementation have traditionally been a "manual" affair because governments' interaction with their citizens has been conducted by human beings like tax collectors, officials, bureaucrats, and civil servants. In the era of e-government, this is no longer necessary, as citizens interact with their governments primarily by electronic means. Information can be easily collected and disseminated and behaviors encouraged or discouraged using rewards and penalties that take immediate effect. Governments will increasingly devise policies using AI that analyzes huge volumes of data and models along with different complex scenarios to find the most effective course of action to deliver the desired result. We can monitor policy implementation in real time and make automatic adjustments.

Analysts can look at the effects of policy across many dimensions, such as how education policies affect health and well-being, how taxation policies impact economic growth, how transportation policies influence people's choice of housing, and how street lighting affects crime rates. The unbiased, superfast calculations of an AI-driven "civil service" will reveal previously unnoticed patterns of behaviors and use that new information to make ingenious and unthought-of new policies and adjustments. "Policy kits" can be made available to developing nations, offering tried and tested solutions to common problems and opportunities.

CHAPTER 11

NAVIGATING THE LABYRINTH OF AI AND PUBLIC POLICY

S O, WHERE DO WE GO FROM HERE? IN THE INTRI-
cate realm of public policy, where decisions reverberate across societies, a technological revolution is quietly unfolding. Artificial intelligence has rapidly traversed the chasm between the theoretical and the tangible, transforming the very fabric of governance.

While developing this book, which encompassed a public policy post-graduate program, multiple methods existed to demonstrate the interconnected nature of technology and policy development. When I handed in my final thesis on open data implications on nation-states, I had extensively made an argument that the liberalization of datasets would show a nearly clear-cut case of correlation between data openness and positive economic activity.

From a policy perspective, my argument was that states needed to do more to enable data-driven policy development. This would be bound to an open-data model that focused on the societal inclusion of key economic datasets to help generate socioeconomic opportunities for growth within a state. My general premise was that if states stifled this element of participation, lower positive economic impacts to states would be the result. I'm paraphrasing a more detailed version of the thesis, but one point I made in my paper was the limited scope of my research in analyzing states with a wider array of parameters to assess their overall open-data adoption.

I had more or less completed my first (of many) final manuscripts for this book, thinking it might be the right time to get on the path of publishing it.

I submitted my final dissertation on October 18, 2022. To my surprise, toward the end of November, OpenAI released ChatGPT, a chatbot platform based on their generative pre-trained transformers (GPT) large language model that had been under development since 2018. As imagined, I realized this book might have already become out of date. But it was also a pivotal moment for the topics highlighted in the book, confirming my premise on the future of public governance.

This final chapter comprises some of my initial thoughts on the labyrinthine world of AI and its profound potential to impact public policy, while also examining its transformative ethical dilemmas and the delicate balance between innovation and prudence. While this is not a comprehensive analysis of case studies, since we are on the cusp of major developments, I hope to cover some key areas that need to be considered in this brave new world. I wrote this final chapter fittingly during a business trip in Singapore, approximately a year after ChatGPT was publicly released.

THE ASCENDANT ROLE OF AI IN PUBLIC POLICY

Throughout the book, I have highlighted how public policy, the bedrock of societal order and cultural progress, has long been intertwined with technological advancements. From the printing press to the rise of the internet, technology has reshaped the landscape of governance without pause. AI, and more specifically, language learning models (LLMs) represent the latest incarnation of technological ingenuity. Introducing generative AI and LLM-based artificial intelligence truly presents a watershed moment in this evolutionary process.

A confluence of factors, including the exponential growth of data, the increasing sophistication of algorithms, and the democratization of AI tools, has propelled AI to the forefront of public policy discourse. AI's ability to process vast quantities of data, identify patterns, and make predictions has opened new frontiers for policymaking.

The potential to enhance data-driven decision-making with a near-laser-focused view of solutions has never been as close as it is today. What is more at play is the removal of various barriers to entry to smaller, less developed states so they too can leverage these new enabling technologies to their fullest socioeconomic potential. While governance will always be a key enabler of this, we cannot deny that these new emerging technologies—if done right—could create situations that I think will change the status quo.

ENHANCING DECISION-MAKING AND RESOURCE ALLOCATION

AI's transformative potential lies in its ability to augment human capabilities and provide policymakers with unprecedented insights and tools to navigate complex societal challenges. AI can sift through mountains of data to extract hidden patterns and relationships that would otherwise remain elusive. This enhanced data-driven approach to policymaking promises to improve decision-making processes, leading to more informed and effective policies. Previous case studies have shown how this can work, but with the support of robust LLMs, multiple catalysts and accelerated insights for decision-making are on the horizon.

What's in store is the ability to further optimize resource allocation by identifying areas where resources are underutilized or misallocated with a far greater level of accuracy. More importantly, we can then focus these insights to ensure potential actions have run through multiple scenarios. By analyzing data on resource distribution, governments can pinpoint inefficiencies and guide policymakers toward more fair and effective resource-allocation strategies.

ETHICAL CONSIDERATIONS: NAVIGATING THE MORAL MAZE

While all of this holds immense promise, its integration into public policy is not without ethical challenges. AI algorithms, if not carefully designed and monitored, can perpetuate existing biases in data, leading to discriminatory outcomes in policy decisions. The "black box" nature of AI algorithms can also hinder transparency, making it perplexing to understand the rationale behind certain outcomes and hold systems accountable. In these instances, LLMs that have a more open framework can address some of the key integrity and analytical bias challenges that are still an area of concern with their adoptions.

The collection and storage of vast amounts of personal data for AI training raises concerns about privacy and the potential for misuse. Policymakers must establish robust data protection measures to safeguard individual privacy and prevent the mishandling of personal data. While many might point to regulation as the key solution to some of these issues, we should also consider the use of AI for these purposes. States can better serve themselves by not over-enforcing AI development and innovation since, as many previous technological advancements have shown, legislation can be slow to adapt to the variables involved.

To harness the benefits of AI—while mitigating its risks—policymakers must embrace responsible AI development and regulation. This entails establishing clear ethical guidelines, promoting transparency, understanding AI algorithms, and ensuring robust data protection measures. Governments must also foster collaboration between technologists, policymakers, and the public to ensure that AI is developed and used responsibly and ethically. Open dialogue and public engagement are essential to building trust and ensuring that AI aligns with societal values.

AI is already making its mark on various facets of public policy. Predictive policing algorithms are used to expect crime hotspots, enabling targeted police deployment and crime prevention strategies. In healthcare, AI is assisting in the diagnosis of diseases such as cancer and diabetic retinopathy by analyzing medical images and providing diagnostic recommendations. AI is also used to detect fraudulent activity in insurance, finance, and government benefits. Imagine the power of having AI policy chatbots that could correlate multiple datasets and provide a very sound and nuanced (and localized) response to the challenges faced by lawmakers today.

THE END STATE

As AI continues to evolve, its impact on public policy will only intensify. AI-driven policymaking, augmented decision-making, and AI-enabled public services will revolutionize the way governments operate and interact with citizens. While policy is a domain primarily led by various stakeholders across a spectrum of communal participation, the inclusion of what would be "non-human" elements into the discourse would almost certainly be accompanied by many forms of speculation and cynicism. This is to be expected and welcomed. The very value creation that is possible requires even the most critical commentators to dissect and engage with the topic. The flip side is this may bring about the overall societal change that is often supported by most progressive parties.

We will never know how to become a better form of ourselves without taking key risks. What is required is an understanding of AI and its key strengths and weaknesses, and not over-idolizing its potential successes. This way, stakeholders—the constituents who ultimately should and will benefit from these policies are not oversold.

AI will inextricably link the coming public policy future. The path forward demands a delicate balance between innovation and prudence, one that ensures that AI serves as a tool for progress and not a catalyst for unintended consequences. It also deserves our undying attention, since this can be the way society progresses forward into a new era of autonomous governance.

ACKNOWLEDGEMENTS

Writing this book, my first, has been quite a journey. What started as a thesis-like paper evolved over three years into a book I can share with everyone. Throughout this journey, I have been fortunate to receive sincere support from people who wholeheartedly backed everything I did to see this personal project through.

To my lovely wife, Nesma, who has been my greatest supporter and advocate in everything I do. You are the single most important factor in enabling me to get this together, and involving our two beautiful sons, Zayed, and Sultan, along with me.

To my parents, my mother and father, you have been the bedrock of my existence and my successes in life. Thank you for being the great parents I aspire to emulate always.

To my brother, Ahmed, for being the most intelligent and well-informed member in my inner circle.

To my other siblings, Khalid, Mona, and Musa, please take note.

A special mention as well to Sultan Al Darmaki, who, while not of the policy ilk, always provided interesting commentary along the way.

I also want to thank Jonathan Gifford, a great mentor and supporter in this book. I only hope I have made this work something you would be proud of.

To Dr. Mark Powell, who was the first person to respond and collaborate his rich experiences into this work, thank you for giving my work a chance.

To my dear friend, Lauri Almann, a man who I have learned so much from over my career, and who I have had the great fortune of staying connected with. Your friendship and mentorship are something I value to this day.

A special thanks to my family within the Abu Dhabi Executive Office, and greater Abu Dhabi government of which I am serving, as of the time of this book's release. This book, while a personal work of mine, resulted from the interactions with key policy leaders who had helped to enable me to reach this personal milestone. I am fortunate to have been among inspirational leaders who are propelling my home, Abu Dhabi, to its greatest potential to the world.

FURTHER READING

BOOKS

Eubanks, Virginia. *Automating Inequality: How High-Tech Tools Profile, Police, and Punish the Poor.* New York: St. Martin's Press, 2018.

Fukuyama, Francis. *Identity: The Demand for Dignity and the Politics of Resentment.* New York: Farrar, Straus and Giroux, 2018.

O'Neil, Cathy. *Weapons of Math Destruction: How Big Data Increases Inequality and Threatens Democracy.* New York: Crown, 2016.

Pasquale, Frank. *The Black Box Society: The Secret Algorithms That Control Money and Information.* Cambridge, MA: Harvard University Press, 2015.

ARTICLES

Bollier, David. *Artificial Intelligence and the Good Society*. Washington, DC: The Aspen Institute, 2019.

Villasenor, John. "Artificial Intelligence, Geopolitics, and Information Integrity." The Brookings Institution, January 30, 2020. https://www.brookings.edu/articles/artificial-intelligence-geopolitics-and-information-integrity/

www.ingramcontent.com/pod-product-compliance
Lightning Source LLC
Chambersburg PA
CBHW031145020426
42333CB00013B/520